Becoming a Parent

Because your family matters . . .

The Wiley *Family Matters* series highlights topics that are important to the everyday lives of family members. Each book tackles a common problem or difficult situation, such as teenage troubles, new babies or problems in relationships, and provides easily understood advice from authoritative professionals. The *Family Matters* series is designed to provide expert advice to ordinary people struggling with everyday problems and bridges the gap between the professional and client. Each book also offers invaluable help to practitioners as extensions to the advice they can give in sessions, and helps trainees to understand the issues clients face.

Titles in the series:

Becoming a Parent

The Emotional Journey Through Pregnancy and Childbirth

Jackie Ganley

John Wiley & Sons, Ltd

Other Wiley Editorial Offices

John Wiley & Sons Inc., 111 River Street, Hoboken, NJ 07030, USA

Jossey-Bass, 989 Market Street, San Francisco, CA 94103-1741, USA

Wiley-VCH Verlag GmbH, Boschstr. 12, D-69469 Weinheim, Germany

John Wiley & Sons Australia Ltd, 33 Park Road, Milton, Queensland 4064, Australia

John Wiley & Sons (Asia) Pte Ltd, 2 Clementi Loop #02-01, Jin Xing Distripark, Singapore 129809

John Wiley & Sons Canada Ltd, 22 Worcester Road, Etobicoke, Ontario, Canada M9W 1L1

Wiley also publishes its books in a variety of electronic formats. Some content that appears in print may not be
available in electronic books.

Library of Congress Cataloging-in-Publication Data
Ganley, Jackie.
  Becoming a parent : the emotional journey through pregnancy and childbirth / Jackie
Ganley.
    p. cm. – (Family matters)
  Includes bibliographical references and index.
  ISBN 0-470-86090-1 (pbk. : alk. paper)
  1. Pregnancy–Psychological aspects. 2. Childbirth–Psychological aspects. 3. Mothers–
Psychology. I. Title. II. Family matters (John Wiley & Sons)
    RG560.G366 2004
    155.6′463–dc22

                                                              2004003365

British Library Cataloguing in Publication Data
A catalogue record for this book is available from the British Library

ISBN 0-470-86090-1

Typeset in 10/12pt Imprint by Dobbie Typesetting Ltd, Tavistock, Devon
Printed and bound in Great Britain by TJ International Ltd, Padstow, Cornwall
This book is printed on acid-free paper responsibly manufactured from sustainable forestry
in which at least two trees are planted for each one used for paper production.

For my mother

CAERPHILLY COUNTY BOROUGH COUNCIL	
CCBD335868	14.01.07
	£12.99

Contents

About the author

Jackie Ganley is a Clinical Psychologist with the South London and Maudsley NHS Trust. She has worked in primary health care with GPs, health visitors, midwives and psychiatric nurses for a number of years. She has two young children.

Preface

The beginning of our journey

My own journey into pregnancy and childbirth began many years before I had children myself. As a newly qualified clinical psychologist, in my first job, I saw many women who were distressed and struggling with their life and so often their problems were to do with the struggle of being a parent. As one father said to me, 'Why doesn't someone write a rule book and just make it easier for all of us?' Well, I soon realised that there was no rule book but many common themes did emerge: the juggling of responsibilities, the loneliness of women cut off from their former life, the sense of losing your identity and balancing your adult needs against the usually more immediate needs of your baby.

One woman whose story I have never forgotten was Sylvia, who was referred for help with depression. Sylvia was in her late sixties and said her life had been dominated by periods of depression and now she felt her final years were slipping away from her. Sylvia said she had always been depressed but when she thought about it, the depression had begun following the birth of her second child. Sylvia said she had rarely allowed herself to think back over that time since she felt embarrassed and ashamed about what had happened. She could remember little of the detail of her labour except that an emergency Caesarean had been necessary. Sylvia remembered feeling distraught and terrified after she had come round from the anaesthetic and she said it seemed like an eternity before she was allowed to see her son. Her husband was at home looking after their daughter and was only allowed to see them during visiting hours. Sylvia said that she had developed an 'illness' while in hospital which had caused her to sweat and shake for no reason. This illness had made her avoid the midwives, as she was terribly embarrassed. During the night Sylvia couldn't sleep and would lie awake wondering if her baby was safe in the nursery and if she was going to survive until the morning. Thus, Sylvia said the midwives clearly thought she was 'odd' and had moved her into a side room away from all the other mothers. Sylvia says she remembers the doctors talking about her on ward rounds but no one ever explained what was happening and so she became convinced she had a serious illness and began to worry that she would die and leave two children without a mother. Sylvia was surprised when a smiling doctor discharged her without warning. On returning home Sylvia felt she had had a lucky escape and although she was relieved, as the weeks went on she just couldn't seem to find the energy that she used to have and the care of the children seemed an enormous burden. Sylvia had moved to their home on marrying her husband and although she knew many local mothers to 'say hello to', she hadn't really made any friends in her new surroundings. She wondered why she wasn't like other mothers who seemed to take everything in their stride.

Sylvia was genuinely surprised to discover that her feelings were not unusual for women who had experienced a complicated delivery. She was particularly amazed to discover that her symptoms were anxiety symp-toms: she had heard of post-natal depression but didn't realise that very many types of emotional reaction are common to having a baby. Sylvia had experienced little support and care from the professionals around her and, like many women of her generation, she was somewhat isolated from other new parents. It seemed heart-breaking that 40 years after having her baby, Sylvia was still trying to understand exactly what had happened to her.

We can learn a great deal from Sylvia's experience about the sort of care and support that women need when they have a baby. It is important to understand what is happening to you and your baby throughout your pregnancy and childbirth. Medical professionals involved in your care should explain exactly what is happening and why, and parents should be encouraged to ask questions and make their own decisions. New parents today are perhaps more aware of the psychological struggles that surround becoming a parent but often during a period of such rapid adjustment it is difficult to take in what is happening. At times, most parents will feel like Sylvia that there is something wrong with them and that the rest of the world appears to know what they are doing!

There are many books on the market that take us through the process of becoming pregnant and giving birth and this information is an important part of our journey. However, this book will not go into detail about the physical process of pregnancy but will concentrate on the emotional transition that takes place. Psychologists often talk about 'life events' as the significant building blocks that form our lives. These can be both positive and negative: getting married, moving house, changing career, bereavement, illness, and so forth. The more of these events you experience at one time, the more likely it is that you will feel pressurised, stressed or depressed. Becoming a parent is probably the biggest transition that many of us will make. So many things change: there are new roles to learn, new responsibilities to take on and parts of the old self to be given up. This is true for both mothers-to-be and fathers-to-be. Women also have to cope with the physical realities of pregnancy: a changing body shape, morning sickness and sometimes serious health complications such as raised blood pressure. Labour and birth also pose new challenges and experiences. As was the case for Sylvia, often the physical consequences of labour can lead to physical and emotional trauma.

Our journey, however, begins with *deciding to have a baby*. There may be no right way to decide but it is certainly an issue that many people spend many hours pondering. You may already be pregnant when you read this book but the decision to become pregnant is often revisited once pregnant: why did we do it? Why don't I feel so certain now? Chapter 2 looks at conception. The area of conception and problems with conception probably merits an entire book and here the issues of the pain and disappointment of fertility problems are only touched upon.

The main section of the book, Chapters 3 and 4, is about *pregnancy*. Pregnancy is usually thought of in terms of three trimesters and the development of the baby in this time. This book will look at the 'psychological stages' of pregnancy. How might you feel in those early weeks? What sorts of worries do newly pregnant women have? How do they cope with morning sickness or cut down their alcohol intake? The middle of pregnancy can be a somewhat different time emotionally. Most women have accepted the pregnancy and are getting used to their new identity of 'pregnant woman'. The focus therefore shifts away from the internal to the external: How can I prepare for this baby? How will my life change? As pregnancy draws to a close, some of the fears of early pregnancy may return. Predominantly these tend to be fears about labour and giving birth. As the pregnancy comes to an end, it is time to disengage from former responsibilities and reinvest in the new future.

However, every pregnancy is different and for some the experience of pregnancy can be overwhelmed by other problems and concerns.

Depression is just as common in pregnancy as it is post-natally. A great deal of attention is given to supporting mothers so that they do not get depressed following the birth of their baby but more attention should in fact be given to identifying problems in pregnancy and supporting women who are depressed or struggling. After all, there is much more time in pregnancy than there will be after the baby is born: time to think, to talk and to begin to make changes. It is all too easy to get wrapped up in the practical plans for the baby.

Chapter 5 on *birth* looks at some of the practical decisions to be made in pregnancy such as, shall I have a hospital or home birth? Labour is then considered: what does it feel like and how can I manage the pain? What are birth partners supposed to do? There is also discussion in this chapter and Chapter 3 of loss during pregnancy and birth.

Many books on pregnancy trail off after the discussion of giving birth and this may be because most books are read in pregnancy and it may just be too difficult to think so far ahead or imagine what the challenges will be when your baby is here. It is, however, better to approach this time from a position of some preparation and therefore there are two further chapters: *the first few days* (Chapter 6) and *the first six weeks* (Chapter 7). The chapters are divided this way since these two time periods seem to be significant. In the first few days new parents are faced with enormous physical and psychological challenges. A new mother has to recover from the experience of labour while at the same time being thrown immediately into the task of parenting. If you were climbing a mountain, you would rest before working your way back down but recovery from labour has to fit in around your new baby. Chapter 6 also discusses the feelings and reactions of the first few days which may be very different to how you might feel after six weeks. In those early days you might experience the baby blues and struggle to do very much at all. However, in the first six weeks mother and baby start to get to know each other and remarkably by six weeks most new parents feel like they have been through a lifetime with their baby and usually feel that they have 'become parents'. At the very least they will have recognised the basic needs of new babies: feeding and sleeping dispersed with moments of crying and being held. Things may still be very chaotic and difficult at the end of the first six weeks but usually the direction seems a little clearer.

For some women, however, the chaos is all that they see. By six weeks a significant number of women are depressed and feel that they are not coping. Chapter 8, therefore, offers some suggestions on how to deal with anxiety and depression, while the final chapter, Chapter 9, looks forward to the future.

Each chapter includes a 'who can help' section to direct you towards appropriate support. There are also discussion points. These are not a definitive guide, just some suggestions to help encourage discussion between parents-to-be. For new parents 'communication, communication, communication' is probably the key to survival. Try to discuss your thoughts, feelings and dilemmas with whoever is around to listen: partner, parent, friend or fellow new parent. Use the various professionals around you to get information and support too. Remember the things that they are interested in may not be your concerns. Most importantly, try to listen to and learn from your interactions with your baby and remember he is unique and will not behave in the same way as other people's babies do.

Throughout the book I have tried to use the stories of families that I have worked with to highlight the struggles that we all face in becoming parents. To protect the identities of those concerned I have changed the names and details of people's stories. I have also taken the decision to refer to babies as 'he' and 'him' throughout. I'm sorry if this offends but as I am the mother of two sons, it was always 'he' in our household and this seemed easier for me. I have also written this book to be read by both mothers-to-be and fathers-to-be and I hope this doesn't alienate the single parent reader. Often new fathers find it far more difficult to become involved in what is happening and it would be ideal if both parents-to-be were to read this book. Support does not necessarily need to come from a father but new parents do far better when they have the concerned support of others. Hopefully, this book can provide you with a little bit of concerned support.

Acknowledgements

A number of people have made it possible for me to write this book but my greatest debt is to James, Jake and George who have disappeared to the park on rainy afternoons and allowed me some time to write. They have been a great source of inspiration in my life and I owe them a great deal in very many ways. Thanks also to my friends and their children who have been with me in my own transition to parenthood and helped to make it such a great journey.

I would like to thank everyone at Wiley for helping this book to come together and also Dr Jane Ogden for her initial suggestion that I should write it.

There are many people who have influenced my professional development over the years and I would like to take this opportunity to thank them. Most of all, I could not have written this book without the numerous people who have shared their own life stories with me over the years. I am very grateful for all I have learned from working with you.

Deciding on parenthood

What are we letting ourselves in for?

The mess, the chaos, the disruption, the expense, the loss of personal space! So why do we do it! Having children is for many people the single most important experience/event of their lives. For many prospective parents it is an irreplaceable part of how they want their lives to be. It may bring great joy and personal fulfilment or it may bring challenges, conflict and sadness at times. For some, the prospect of children is daunting and certainly not an inevitable choice: to have children will be a decision they consciously make after much exploration of their feelings and motives. For others, pregnancy is a situation they collide with – an unexpected event possibly in a less than ideal situation. For increasing numbers of people today children will arrive with a new relationship itself where the partner is a single parent.

More and more people today are seeing child-rearing as a choice and not a biological inevitability. For those living in the wealthy nations of the world, parenting has become a lifestyle choice. Having children has enormous financial, emotional and social implications. Whatever the position of prospective parents, whether married for years, a single person, teenagers, or a couple with fertility problems, all will find themselves financially worse off, emotionally challenged and having to give up (if only temporarily) many of the social pleasures that make life manageable. Clearly, deciding to have children is not a particularly rational decision and if we really sat down and calculated the financial burden, the heartache and the sleepless nights, then most people would probably decide against reproduction. So why does it continue to be a choice that the majority will make?

Calling this chapter 'Deciding on parenthood' might be misleading: it is here because it is a subject that many people spend hours thinking about. This chapter's aim is not to give the impression that there is a right way to decide or a list of questions that you can go through and come up with the right answer: 'yes, it's for me' or 'no, I'm better suited to my career'. At its most basic, deciding whether or not to have children is about weighing up the balance between our adult needs and our perception of the needs and demands of any potential children. However, it is almost impossible to predict the 'costs' of children for any particular individual. One might begin to reckon up the specific financial burden but it is very difficult to predict the emotional costs, especially as these are specific to each individual. Even after the initial decision to become pregnant, the decision-making continues. Having had a first child, it is still a big decision for many parents about whether and when to have number two . . . or three . . . or four.

One might argue that it is perhaps a reflection of a more 'responsible' society that people are sitting down and thinking about whether they would make good parents. There are few people left who still believe that 'God decides' whether a baby is born but there is an alternative view that we have become incredibly omnipotent and unrealistic about how much control we actually have over life and making new life. This chapter will take a look at some of the factors that are involved in making this decision.

What does it mean to be a family?

Most of us probably don't stop to think about what a family is. The family that we grew up in probably influences our picture of a typical family. Large numbers of us grew up in a situation where there was a mother and a father who were married, with two or three children and our mother stayed at home in the early years of our life. The family has obviously changed over recent years. Separation and divorce are far more common and now having a baby, as a single parent, is no longer seen as a shameful mistake. The single parent household is now said to be the largest growing new household type. The politicians of the Right like to argue that the 'traditional family' has broken down and that its values have been lost too. It is interesting to wonder what the traditional family actually is, or was, and whether there has ever been a static family structure that was such a defining force in our society.

A look at our social history will show that the family has always been evolving and changing, especially in the past hundred years. In the mid-twentieth century sociologists talked about the rise of the nuclear family and the demise of the traditional extended family. Now we are told that the nuclear family is breaking down as we have the rise of the single parent household. How long the extended family existed is unclear, since life was such that extended families could not have been common 500 years ago.

It seems likely that family structures have changed as societies have evolved and our needs for survival have changed. Taking just the history of British society and the number of wars that were fought in the last millennium, it is likely that single parent families were very much the norm. One has only to look at the history of the past century with two world wars to see that for extended periods of time fathers were absent from the home, many never to return and that women had to leave their children in the care of others while they worked in factories or on the land. Working mothers were not created in the 1990s.

So what does the family look like today? If diversity is a good thing, then the family is probably doing very well! In this country most babies today are still born to couples but the long-term prospects for those couples is poor in terms of divorce and separation. The break-up of the couple before the child becomes an adult (even where the separation is sensitively handled and the couple continue reasonable relations) does have consequences for the child. These children are more likely to have emotional or behavioural difficulties but this is not inevitable and there are many influences on a child's development. These issues have to be balanced against the costs to the parent of remaining in the relationship, especially where one partner may be experiencing stress or violence.

Just when we might think the nuclear family unit is doomed, however, there are new types of nuclear families coming to take its place. Many more gay and lesbian couples are now openly becoming nuclear family units through assisted conception or adoption and fostering. Many couples who previously would not have had children are doing so through fertility treatment. The largest new group is said to be the single parent household. However, statistics can be misleading and it is probably only a small number of these families that remain static throughout the life of the child. The 'reconstituted family', where one family is formed from other family units, is becoming much more common.

From a broader social perspective many Western societies are predicting that their populations are shrinking dramatically as not enough children are being born to replace the population. This is a complex issue since populations do not necessarily expand in expected ways. Often the more prosperous a society becomes, the fewer children people will have. Other societies struggle to contain a growing population. So the family today comes in many shapes and sizes probably just as it has always done.

Betty and Peter's story

Betty came to see me after a year of feeling depressed: at times it was so severe she could hardly speak. Her husband Peter said he couldn't understand it since they had looked forward to retirement and they certainly had enough money to manage. Betty had retired from her job as a cleaner some years ago and had looked forward to a retirement spent with her grandchildren. Betty was the oldest of 11 children and had helped to raise her brothers and sisters following the death of her mother. Betty said she loved children but had only had two because things were different in the years after the war and they couldn't afford any more. Her son had emigrated to Australia with his family and her daughter was married to a soldier and they were currently living in Germany. Betty said she felt 'completely useless', had nothing to do with her time and that her house was empty unless the family were visiting. She said she would never expect her children not to lead their own lives but she felt 'life was empty without your family around you'.

What does it mean to be a mother? Changes for women

Social roles such as 'mother' or 'shopkeeper' or 'friend' are governed by certain rules or expectations. The role of 'mother' has changed drastically in the past hundred years and has probably always been changing in terms of the needs of the wider society at a particular time. For example, during the wars of the past century women were expected to maintain the supply of food and products, especially munitions, that would keep society functioning in time of war. Often they also had to accept long separations from their children who were evacuated for safety. Much has been written about how in the 1950s post-war propaganda (including psychological research) was used to draw women back into the home as full-time parents so that the men returning from war would have jobs. Ideas persisted that children could be 'damaged' by the absence of their mother. However, society has currently swung again towards accepting women in the workplace and there is censure for those who stay at home and claim benefits to bring up their children. It may be that in our current society supporting children financially is seen as more important than supporting them emotionally.

The role of 'mother' is therefore ever changing and this uncertainty for society about what exactly a mother is can make it more difficult for the individual woman to assume the role. This may add to or generate a sense of insecurity in late pregnancy. What exactly does it mean to become a mother? Is a mother someone who works outside of the home? Do mothers go clubbing? Do they instinctively know how to care for a newborn baby? In effect, women construct for themselves the role of 'mother', being influenced both by the wider society and their own needs, preferences and responses to their baby. Your early interactions with the baby will shape your perception of yourself as a mother: if your baby is born of very low birth weight your experience will be very different to a mother who gives birth to a 9 lb baby. Your view of yourself as a mother is not static: it will change as you have good times and bad times and as your child displays different needs and demands.

John and Rosemary's story

Rosemary came for help with depression the roots of which seemed to stem from dealing with her three-year-old son. Alex seemed a very active and healthy boy but he ate hardly anything throughout the day, which caused his parents an enormous amount of anxiety. John and Rosemary had married early in their twenties and had hoped to have children but the years had rolled on with nothing happening. They had approached their doctor but initial tests revealed no reasons for their not conceiving and they decided to 'wait and see'. After 13 years they were finally rewarded with a healthy baby boy. Rosemary admitted that they had found the adaptation to parenthood enormously difficult. Their lives had become very ordered and predictable over their married life and now they had sleepless nights, tantrums and constant mess around the house. Rosemary felt guilty about feeling angry with Alex at times and realised that she let him 'get away with everything' for an easy life. Rosemary gradually began setting some limits for Alex and was amazed to find that life for everyone in the family improved.

How did having children become a choice?

It is unlikely that our grandparents ever stopped to consider whether they *wanted* to have children. For our grandmothers, making sure that children occurred within wedlock, i.e. some sort of contract to support them and their offspring, was their main concern. So what has turned child-rearing into a choice? The development of the contraceptive pill in the mid-twentieth century has perhaps done more than any other factor to create the idea of parenting as a choice. With the arrival of the pill came the arrival of the belief that we could decide when we wanted children, how many we wanted and whether we wanted them at all. So society no longer believed that it was God's decision or that it was a biological inevitability. However, there are other changing social factors that have contributed to people seeing having children as a choice. In recent years the role of women in the workplace has been changing rapidly. Women have always worked, despite what some would have us believe, but increasingly women are seeing their career as lifelong, something that children must be assimilated into, rather than just 'something to do until you get married'. As the dimensions of the workforce continue to change, in many areas women now find themselves the only reliable earner. As service and part-time jobs increase for women in areas of high unemployment, many men, skilled in a particular trade, find themselves unemployable. The possibility of children is financially challenging, as there will be no 'reliable' wage.

At the other end of the financial spectrum many couples today are deciding that their lives are complete without children: the high social and personal costs outweigh the 'biological' desire to reproduce. Couples, and women in particular, can feel that their lives are full enough and that having a child is all about what they will have to give up rather than feeling there is a great void to fill. Prosperity paradoxically makes us more aware of the costs of children.

But despite contraception and education and various life options, how many of us really choose to have a baby? How many of us really decide? Are not a large number of children conceived by 'accident' whereby there has been a significant enough psychological shift for the couple, such that the scales have shifted more in the direction of 'yes' to children than 'no'? However, some pregnancies do arrive very much by accident and then the decision-making begins.

Kara's story

Kara came to see me for help with an eating disorder. She tended to diet and then binge on alcohol and food. She would use laxatives and vomit when she sobered up. In the course of our sessions Kara became pregnant. (She had been using the contraceptive pill, which is clearly not recommended as a contraceptive for women with such eating problems.) The father was her flatmate and they had had a 'fling' during a drinking binge. From what looked like a disastrous situation Kara was able to decide that she needed to take control of her life and sort out her problems in a different way. The pregnancy helped her to get some control over her eating problems. She struggled greatly but accepted the idea of eating regular meals and the binging decreased very quickly. Her flatmate helped her to cut down on her drinking but he was not keen on becoming a father. Kara suddenly decided to return home to her parents in Argentina and I did not see her again.

The tasks of parenting

What do children need?

So if we are deciding to have children as a positive choice, then what is it we are deciding to take on? What will our new responsibilities be and how will these impinge on our adult life? Just as much as adult life is continually evolving so is childhood. It is clear that the nature of *parenting* has changed radically in the past hundred years and probably greatly in the past generation. Parenting is no longer primarily about finding food and shelter. The emphasis of bringing up children today is much more *child-centred*. The time that we spend with our children is no longer just incidental or about supervision, it is expected now to be about 'playing' and 'teaching' and 'talking to'. It is potentially much more 'difficult' to be a parent as the tasks have increased and become more psychologically complex. Although many of our grandparents struggled against great poverty and adversity just to keep their children alive, it is hard to compare parenting today and say that it is easier. It is clearly different. Our children are growing up in a very complex social world and helping them to negotiate their way in it is difficult, particularly when we may still be struggling to find our own direction. There are lots of expectations of children in our society and consequently they need a great deal of support and specific guidance.

Children today start formal education and are subject to testing much earlier than in the past. A generation ago nursery 'education' was about playing for a couple of hours separate from mum. Now there are early learning goals to be 'achieved'. School children also have greater access to ideas and information via television and the Internet. They are also subject to advertising specifically targeted at them.

So parents today are expected to play, to educate, to support and to guide in a way that they probably did not experience with their own parents. They must also set boundaries or rules for their children without smacking (by the time this book is published the government may be debating legislation on making corporal punishment illegal). It is not surprising really when we look at the pressures on families that children are increasingly suffering from 'mental health problems' and being diagnosed as having an attention deficit/hyperactivity disorder 'ADHD'.

Lucy and Johnny's story

Lucy came for help with her six-year-old son Johnny who was difficult to manage, especially at bedtime. Lucy was a single parent and was working full-time in order to make sure that Johnny did not suffer financially from the absence of a supportive father. She had secured for Johnny a place at a very good private school and he was doing extremely well for his age. Johnny, however, was refusing to go to bed at night and would keep coming back down stairs and would be tired and argumentative in the mornings. When we considered Johnny's routine, however, it was clear that from 7 in the morning when he left home for school, right through until 6.30 when he arrived home, he was the model of good behaviour. Clearly he was actually doing extremely well, it was just that Lucy only saw bad behaviour which spoilt their time together. It was hard for Lucy to accept that Johnny was doing well because she felt that she had to be perfect or people would criticise her since she was a single parent. However, she decided to put him to bed half-an-hour later than she would have liked and to spend that time playing 'rough-and-tumble' games with Johnny. Bedtimes improved immediately.

Should I go back to work and how will it affect my child?

Most women today are working when they contemplate having a baby or find themselves pregnant unexpectedly. The issues about whether to return to work or how your working life might be different when you have a child are uppermost in the minds of most women when contemplating having a family. When the prospect of having children is some way off, then it is perhaps not clear how your life will change: it is only through the experience of being pregnant and becoming a parent that one can really know how their feelings and responsibilities will change. The balancing act of work and children changes over the course of the child's or children's life too, as their needs differ and your situation evolves. Consequently it is impossible to have *all* the decisions made beforehand. We will return to these issues in later chapters but as well as what is right for you as an individual, women are also interested to know about the research evidence regarding women, work and the possible consequences for their children.

There is currently great debate on whether a mother returning to work during a child's early years is detrimental to the child's health and development. It would be difficult to give a simple answer to this, so instead a few points will be highlighted here to give a flavour of the debate. There is evidence to show that some children do less well emotionally if their mothers work before they are a year old, if they work full-time or long hours and if the quality of the childcare is poor (see Belsky, 2001). These factors are said to affect infant–parent attachment and this is more often true for boys. There may also be more aggressive and non-compliant behaviour during the pre-school years from these children. However, many have argued that the quality of care is the fundamental factor. Mothering or maternal sensitivity is the best predictor of children's social and emotional development, whether mothers are working or not. With regard to child-care, responsive carers who are warm and interactive and provide opportunities for learning are the key to good outcomes.

The actual amount of time that a working mother today spends interacting with and playing with her child compared to her own stay-at-home grandmother may not be hugely different. After all, the latter would have spent a great deal of time hand-washing nappies, walking to the shops and probably looking after a larger number of children. We should not forget too the changing role of fathers and the role that they might play when a mother returns to work. Probably most fathers are more involved with their children today than they were a generation ago and the concept of leisure time, i.e. doing things together socially as a family, was probably something that happened rarely for our grandparents. All these different factors regarding the availability of support for the parents will affect how a family adapts to a mother returning to work.

When looking at this research, one has to consider the methodological difficulties inherent in such work. For example, when comparing the children of women who have chosen to return to work and the children of women who have not, we are not comparing two similar groups. This does not take into account why women have returned to work or have chosen to stay at home. It may be that some of the differences between the children are part of the reason that the decision to return to work or not was made: your relationship with your baby and the temperament of the child may affect whether you feel returning to work is right for you.

The generalities of research mask the individual stories behind women's decisions about work. For many mothers who are struggling at home with their baby the break from the home may have helped improve the relationship between mother and child. Staying at home in itself will not necessarily make everything all right in your relationship with your child: it depends what you do there. For example, if you are depressed, find it difficult to provide much stimulation for the baby and have little contact with other families, then your toddler may enjoy and benefit from a few hours a week at a nursery.

It would be interesting to research how women make the decision to return to work. Why do some women decide to return and others to stay at home? Is it purely economics or is it to do with the relationship with the baby?; is it to do with beliefs held before the baby arrived and how did these beliefs develop? Having returned to work, why does the situation work for some mothers and not for others? Which factors are better predictors of the parents being happy with the decision and which factors contribute to the situation not working out and having to be changed?

One recent study highlighted that women who in pregnancy expressed more commitment to work and less anxiety about non-family child-care were more likely to have securely attached infants. These types of question might be of more use to mothers than research that tries to dictate whether it is 'right' or 'wrong' to return to work.

How many years will the children depend on me?

The picture that we hold in our heads of 'a family' is defined by the beliefs of the society we live in. In our society today we have to hold the contradiction of the idea that children are 'growing up too quickly' or being 'robbed of their childhood' versus the reality that children are clearly becoming dependent on their parents for much longer. This may be due to the complexities of the task of parenting and of the society that we are preparing children to be independent in. It may just be about economics. More young people are at university and financially dependent for a much longer period of time, particularly in light of trends to get more young people into higher education. Spiralling housing costs keep many more teenagers living at home for much longer periods. These factors interact with cultural practices of particular groups within society, which may determine the situations in which the offspring may or may not live separately. It will be interesting to see how the effects of rising housing costs over recent years affect a generation of young people who are unable to afford to leave home until they are well established in a career. Many observers argue that we have become too over-protective of our children and that we should 'take more risks' in order to help their development.

The needs of parents

Are children in my life plan?

So with all these issues to think about in terms of a child, where does that leave the parent? Are you a parent first or an individual first? What aspects of our adult life are important to us and are these compatible with having children? Just as we now grow up not to see children as an inevitability, we are also likely to have a model in our mind of our 'adult life'. Most of us have expectations that form in adolescence about our education, our employment, our relationships and social life, and so on. Today we are faced by enormous choice. Our relative wealth in the West means that many young people are consumers, and products and lifestyles are intensively marketed at this group. The 'dual-income–no-kids' situation is seen as the financial ideal in terms of access to the best that money can buy: entertainment, designer goods, holidays and housing – all most available to this group. They have both the money and the time to participate. So does becoming a parent mean giving up all of this?

Research shows that some things clearly do change after having a baby. Satisfaction with your relationship tends to decline. This seems to be the case whether your relationship was good or bad to start with. Obviously a good relationship doesn't turn into a terrible one. More likely, issues that have always existed but perhaps been managed before become more significant when you have had sleepless nights and have to care for a very needy and demanding little person. Clearly, too, for most couples today there are work and financial implications involved in child-rearing. Children over time cost an awful lot of money and most families will probably see their earnings decrease since even if you return to the same job you will have child-care costs. Whatever you might think about a baby not changing your life, it does. Work, if you do return, is different if you have a baby to consider. Your social life will change and how you view yourself too.

Should I go back to work and how will it affect me?

If we have at some point definitive research to show that the children of working mothers do less well emotionally, we have to balance this information against research evidence over the past 30 years that shows women who stay at home to care for their children are more vulnerable to depression. In fact, working women suffer less depression than unemployed women who, in turn, fare better than homemakers. This again brings us back to the importance of individual factors: how you feel about returning to work or staying at home, what contribution your partner can make, how flexible your employment situation is and who is available to help you.

The transition to parenthood is not, however, as negative as some of these factors might suggest. The majority of people make the transition and manage to position themselves somewhere along the continuum between totally child-centred and totally individual-centred. It obviously takes different lengths of time and involves different struggles for different people.

Claire and David's story

Claire and David had their first child when they were both in their late thirties. They had both worked in management positions in the same department store for a number of years. They had thought about having children for a number of years and eventually Claire became pregnant following a 'second honeymoon' holiday. Claire found the transition to being at home very difficult and could barely get dressed before the evening in the early weeks. She had a lot of support from her Health Visitor but otherwise rarely saw anyone else during the day and she knew no other mums with babies or young children. Claire became

> *increasingly resentful of David who would come home talking about*
> *events in their office and 'what everybody was getting up to'. She felt*
> *that their lives were now so totally different that there was no point in*
> *talking to him because he couldn't understand. David was aware*
> *things weren't right but didn't know what to do. Problems came to a*
> *head one night when David came home from work to find that Claire*
> *had had a 'clear out' and sent his record collection to a charity shop.*
>
> *In time, Claire and David did come to enjoy their new situation.*
> *Claire started to develop a new life for herself. She began to attend a*
> *mother-and-baby group and made some good friends in time through*
> *a working mothers network.*

Amidst all this choice and individuality certain trends do seem to have emerged to define the family currently: the delaying of having children into the late twenties or early thirties, smaller families, mothers returning to work, and so on. This probably says something about how we are trying to balance these issues. The delaying of children can allow a woman to establish herself in her career, for some financial stability to be achieved and returning to work to provide for both financial and social or intellectual needs. Whether we are more 'mature' in our thirties, i.e. able to delay our own needs while dealing with a child and therefore better parents, or whether we find it even harder to give up the social and financial advantages of being childfree is something of a delicate balance.

But who is going to change?

Where a child is born to a couple, there are clearly issues to negotiate about who is going to change and by how much. Many couples run into problems with the arrival of a child when the assumptions of the partners about who is going to do what are radically different. Many couples, before children, feel that their lives are running along in parallel and that life tasks are shared out, if not equally, at least in a way that is acceptable to both. The arrival of a child throws all this up in the air. The majority of infants have their mother as primary carer and from the beginning the *responsibility* for the baby rests with the mothers. If a mother takes maternity leave and breast-feeds, then quite quickly that pattern becomes firmly established so that she is getting up at night, deciding when the baby should be fed, making plans for child-care, and so on. Clearly, although many women now return to work, it is likely that the mother organises the child-care and does the 'picking up' and 'dropping off'. Many women feel resentful when life for a partner returns to something that looks like his previous life and theirs is in a state of flux.

There is no 'right' way of sharing out the responsibilities, it is a question of how the individuals perceive the sharing of the tasks. What does it mean to both parties for a woman to be 'at home with the baby'? It may bring with it the expectation that the mother takes over the running of the home and that dinner is on the table when the partner gets home. It is perhaps important to keep negotiating and renegotiating who does what. Post-natal depression will be covered in some depth in later chapters but the seeds of later emotional problems are often sown in the decisions that are made, or not made, early on.

Brian and Sarah's story

Brian had run a successful business as an interior designer but when property prices collapsed he could not find work. At this time he had two pre-school children. He came to see me after a year of feeling depressed. He had spent the previous three years at home looking after his two daughters while his wife went out to work as a practice nurse. Brian said he truly enjoyed looking after the children and felt he was making a good job of it. However, he said, under the surface, he felt totally worthless. He found many of the household tasks terribly monotonous and unrewarding. Now that the children were at school he felt he would desperately love to work again but at nearly 50 he felt he was now almost unemployable. His wife Sarah always came home from work 'totally stressed out' and he felt that she resented him for not finding work. He found it very difficult to think that doing a good job with the children was as valuable as doing a 'proper' job. He also missed the camaraderie of workmates and the after-work social life.

Who is going to help?

One important factor in dealing with life events and changes is having help and support from others. This may be a time in our lives when having moved around to pursue career and social needs we return to thoughts of our own families and how they might be able to support us. Where family ties are strong and geographically available, many new parents look to their parents for support or strengthen ties with siblings or other relatives who may be able to provide a variety of types of support: financial, emotional and practical. Earlier we talked of the decline of the extended family and today as many more grandparents are less available, then we are perhaps turning to our friends (often with their own children) and the paid child-care sector to provide support. Many women may in returning to part-time work simply be buying themselves some time away from their child which previous generations may have found more readily available from the extended family.

The influence of society

Society is a very important mediator in the family. So far we have thought only about having children as a free choice but inevitably living in a social group means that the group will decide certain rules about how its members live their lives. Many today believe that we live in a 'nanny state' that increasingly prescribes and legislates about how we should bring up our children and there are certainly areas where the state directly intervenes. Recently a number of measures that direct the lives of the under-fives have come into force. The state provides free nursery places for many three year-olds and all four year-olds. Clearly, the state believes education at an early age is important. In more subtle ways the state is involved with the family early on. It has invested millions of pounds in providing 'Sure Start' in areas of social need. This involves various types of family support for parents of young children. These interventions may be the 'carrot' as alongside this we have the emphasis on 'parental responsibility'. If families do not educate their children they can be fined for the non-attendance of their children at school. Parents whose children's behaviour is out of control can to be sent to 'anger management' or 'parenting' classes when their children are in trouble with the law.

Most would agree that it is the responsibility of a society to educate and train a workforce. However, the state has begun to consider decisions about how we raise our children as seen in the increasing pressure for the state to decide and legislate about corporal punishment or smacking. Although the trend is moving away from smacking, the issue is whether the state should just recommend or whether it should decide (i.e. make it a criminal offence to do so). Perhaps the trend towards legislation rather than information is because the task of parenting seems so complex that we all wish for some rules to guide us. It is easier if someone says this is definitely right or wrong.

We're not all trying to make the same family: atypical and reconstituted families

Just as many couples today are deciding that their lives are complete without children, others are taking on non-stereotypical family situations: becoming a single parent, having a child within a gay or lesbian relationship, or forming a 'reconstituted family' where one family is formed from other family units.

Single parenthood has now become a choice for some rather than a mistake. The rise in the availability of assisted conception has opened up the range of parental opportunities. Women now having babies beyond the menopause, lesbian couples and single women are able to have babies.

Although fewer babies are available for adoption in this country, more children with 'special needs' and older children are being adopted and fostered than was the case previously.

Louise and Ross's story

Louise met Ross when she was 19 years old and quite quickly the relationship developed and they bought a flat together. Ross was divorced and had two boys of seven and five who came to stay most weekends. Louise had a very stressful job in a call centre and often worked extra shifts when Ross could not get carpentry work. Louise had always wanted children but being a weekend mother to two lively boys was quite a tall order for a woman only 20 years old herself. Louise longed to have a baby of her own but Ross felt that they already had the financial and practical responsibility for two children and that they couldn't manage another child. This inevitably led to resentment and Louise often worked at weekends because she felt so angry with the children when they misbehaved. Ross tended to lavish gifts on the children and Louise felt them to be ungrateful and spoilt. Louise intermittently became depressed but could see no way out of the situation.

Isn't the decision different for everyone?

So possibly many of us decide in a rather chaotic way or by just 'seeing what happens' but clearly we are all making the decision from a different starting place. To fall pregnant by accident at 15 is very different to becoming pregnant at 30 or 46. We all approach parenthood from our own unique position, so does that make it more difficult for some than for others?

Social support

Most social studies of depression in women point to being at home looking after a child as putting you at greater risk for psychological ill-health, especially depression. Problems are not inevitable and having readily available forms of social support can be very useful. Ante-natal or parenting classes bring people together with other parents-to-be and these contacts with other people in the same situation are probably more useful than the explicit aims of the group.

Health and disability

Many people may approach having a family with a range of different needs. If you are disabled, you will give extra thought to how you will manage a baby and a growing child and what situations may present particular difficulty. Probably many issues cannot be foreseen, as for able-bodied parents, the issues that one child will present are different to another. You may also be looking into what extra support may be available from the statutory or voluntary bodies.

Emotional well-being

Most people are now aware of the possibility of post-natal depression following the birth of a baby and many try to take steps to have extra help and support at this time. We do, however, tend to overlook the fact that many women become pregnant while experiencing emotional difficulties or these problems develop in the pregnancy. Some women may be depressed, they may have had a manic episode that required hospital treatment, they may be struggling with an eating disorder or dealing with the effects of a difficult relationship: the list is endless. This may be related to the pregnancy in some way: there may be fears about the health of the baby, the pregnancy may have been ill-timed or these psychological difficulties may have been due to external factors: the loss of a job, relationship difficulties, family problems, financial worries, and so on. One could try to time a pregnancy when there are fewer pressures around but it would be almost impossible to plan a pregnancy at a time when everything is stable. Pregnancy lasts for the best part of a year and life around you will continue and many events, for example, bereavement, are out of our control.

How do we view the world?

Having a baby is probably one of the most stressful life events that many of us will deal with. Our life, how we view ourselves and how others see us will radically change. There are social, emotional and financial costs involved in raising children so maybe it is not surprising that it all becomes too much at times and mothers especially are more prone to psychological difficulties. However, being ready to accept and face change and trying to adapt to it make it much more likely that this transition will be successful. Some people seem to adapt to new situations very easily and this seems to be to do with how they view life: the more reluctant you are to embrace change the more difficult you will find it. Generally, I found when working with people, helping them to deal with psychological problems, that the more that a person is willing to embrace new ideas, see things from a different perspective or try out new behaviours or responses, the more likely they are to be able to recover from their symptoms.

Social factors

Unfortunately children do not always arrive into the ideal situation and there can be a conflict between what feels emotionally right and what is practically right. Again, the fact that pregnancy lasts a relatively long time, even if you feel yourself to be in a stable financial and practical position, things can come along during the course of the pregnancy that were unforeseen: redundancy, a housing problem, family crises, all manner of factors can change your readiness to become a parent.

What if I don't become pregnant?

Some couples while deciding on whether or not to have children also begin to consider what they would do if they were unable to conceive. This is probably a time when ideas can only be sounded out in the most general terms since it is rather difficult to look for solutions to this problem before it happens. If you are 20 years old you will have a different view of conception than someone who is trying to get pregnant at 45. The next chapter will look at issues concerning conception.

Who can help?

Deciding about whether or not to have a family is not really something that a professional can help with, it is a personal decision for the prospective parents weighing up their personal circumstances. However, the process of deciding may throw up particular issues for a couple or the individuals. One partner may not wish to have children, while the other does – where does this leave the relationship? An individual may decide 'yes' to children, but not now or not with this person. Contemplating having children may reawaken problems from a troubled childhood that the person feels need to be resolved before children are conceived. Very often people seek help with problems because they want to have children in the foreseeable future and something stands in their way: a drinking problem, obsessive-compulsive problems or relationship conflicts that need resolving.

Talking to your partner or to close friends may be enough to set about making changes yourself but sometimes you may feel you keep falling at the same hurdle. In this case you may feel that professional help is needed. Seeing your GP for general advice is often a good place to start. They can give details of counselling organisations or may even have appropriate services to which you can be referred. There are specific organisations that offer relationship counselling such as 'Relate' that can offer an initial consultation to assess if they can help (see the list of addresses on p. 181).

Most young reasonably healthy adults will probably have seen their GP infrequently in the past and know little about the services available at their surgery. When you become pregnant and over the next few years with a young child, you will find yourself using these services far more often. Therefore, it is really important to have at least one doctor in a group practice that you feel reasonably comfortable with and able to talk to. This is worth thinking about now: find out what your surgery offers in terms of baby clinics, health visitor support, or are all of these facilities located elsewhere?

Discussion points

This chapter could generate endless discussion points so what follows below are only general pointers and you may wish to make your own agenda:

1. If you imagine your life in five years time, what would you like to see? Do you have a child/children? Are you working? Where are you living? Do you and your partner both have similar ideas/expectations?

2. Think of your biggest fears about becoming pregnant/becoming a family. Are these the same for you both? Do they seem insurmountable problems? Are there any solutions or compromises?

3. Which aspects of your life now are the most important to you (e.g. football on Sunday; staying a size 10; promotion at work)? Make a list of things you feel you must have or must do. How do you feel these might be affected by having a family? What could you give up/postpone and what must you have?

2

Conception

Conception: the other side of family planning

If you have struggled with the decision about whether or not to have a baby or when might be the best time, then conception might appear to be the easy part and, for the majority, this is certainly the case. However, for some couples conception itself can be a difficult and uncertain experience.

Contraception and the myth of family planning

It is perhaps true that the success of the contraceptive pill, which brought with it the idea of 'family planning', has contributed to the growth of problems with conception. That is not to suggest any adverse affects from the pill itself, more that the ability to *avoid* conception has created the erroneous belief that we *control* conception. With contraception came the idea of family planning: that couples decide, not 'God' or 'nature', as our grandparents may have believed. These factors set up certain expectations that children will arrive 'when I plan them' or 'when I stop taking the pill'. This, combined with technological/medical advances in assisted conception, has created a climate where we believe we can have babies on demand: timed to fit our life plan, ordered via the Internet if all else fails. How cruel then it is when months roll on and that longed-for pregnancy does not arrive.

Perfect timing?

Clearly, most of us cannot perfectly time a pregnancy since conception cannot reliably be switched 'on and off'. Conception may occur quite some time after we have decided that we want children and anywhere from one month to one year is deemed 'normal'. Perhaps this uncertainty is in fact helpful as it makes us aware from the outset that babies don't just fit in around the rest of your life. If you do get pregnant when you wanted to, you still can't be certain exactly when the baby will arrive: anywhere from 37 to 42 weeks is normal/full-term but some babies arrive earlier. Many couples haven't exactly planned their pregnancy but they are happy when they discover that they are pregnant. This isn't such a bad way to 'time' a baby since it releases you from the pressure of trying to find the 'perfect time'.

So the decision is made in a number of different ways but some trends do seem to be emerging. The age of first-time mothers appears to be getting older. The delaying of childbirth into the late twenties and thirties may partly be due to this sense that we can produce a baby on demand. However, statistically, fertility falls off rapidly in the thirties, especially after 35. Current trends to 'time' pregnancies around our social needs do therefore have associated risks. For the vast majority, family planning works very well in that parents can choose to time their conception when they feel emotionally and financially ready to have a child. However, the biological clock is ticking if you don't become pregnant quickly, and your age may well turn the situation into a problem.

Discovering you are pregnant

That moment of discovering that you are pregnant may not be quite how you imagined. Most women, even those who were desperate to be pregnant, can experience a range of feelings: shock, disbelief, euphoria, tears, all of these may make up your reaction. For some, taking a pregnancy test is a big event that they want to share with their partner. Others may wish to take this step alone or may be uncertain of the involvement of the potential father-to-be. Many women may be fairly sure that they are pregnant but avoid taking a test in order to avoid knowing the result. For some, even after a positive pregnancy test, they may still try to deny the pregnancy until they are ready to deal with the realities of their situation. Partners too may react in unexpected ways: they may be delighted by the news when you had expected them not to be or they may be distant even though you had embarked upon this process together. After the confirmation of the pregnancy by the taking of a test, a process of assimilating the news begins and this journey will continue in the next chapter. For some women, however, conception does not come easily or may not happen at all.

When pregnancy doesn't happen

How long should we expect to wait?
When do I have a problem?

Having made the decision to become pregnant, most of us will have an idea of how long we think that it might take to conceive. This is probably based on what we know from our families and friends or any information we may have gained from books or television. Therefore, to some extent, problems of conception or 'infertility' are self-defined by our expectations. John and Rosemary (whose story was in the last chapter) waited 13 years before their baby arrived; other couples are surprised if a baby is not conceived within the first month of trying. Most specialist medical services will have definitions of fertility problems but clearly a simple definition will not work for every couple. A number of factors are relevant for each individual.

Your age

Clearly, your age will affect your view of the situation. If you are 42, you will be very aware of your declining fertility and if you are determined to have a baby, then you are much more likely to want to investigate whether there is a problem as your chances are decreasing. If you are 23 and leading a very full life, you may be quite willing to wait for a few years before you decide that there is a problem.

Readiness to have a family

However, whatever your age, if you are absolutely set on having a baby, then you may see every period that arrives as an unexplainable failure. Many women expect to get pregnant from the first month of trying. Often in a couple one partner is more uncertain about parenthood and therefore may take much longer to be willing to identify a problem.

Gynaecological history

Other factors may affect your view of your potential fertility. If you have a history of any gynaecological problems, a previous sexually transmitted disease, a previous termination of pregnancy or a previous miscarriage or stillbirth, any of these factors may increase your sense of anxiety if conception does not occur immediately. For most women these anxieties are unjustified and may be the result of guilt about some of these past experiences. However, it may be that you need to discuss your particular situation with your GP to sort out the fact from the fear.

Clearly, a number of highly individual factors will contribute to you viewing yourself as having a problem and it is always worth discussing these feelings with someone you trust. A visit to the GP might be appropriate for you but it does also represent the first step in identifying a 'problem', which can increase your anxiety about the situation. Everyone's expectations are different.

Chloe's story

As a psychologist I am always interested by the information that is given in the referral letters that turn up before you meet the person concerned. I was particularly intrigued when a GP asked me to see Chloe whom he said was depressed because she was unable to fall pregnant. Chloe was just 17 years old at that time. Chloe said she was desperate to get pregnant, her two older sisters both had children and her house was always full of babies as her mother was a child-minder. Chloe did not have a boyfriend and was still a virgin. Chloe said she couldn't get pregnant because she was 'too fat and ugly' and she would never get a boyfriend.

Chloe seemed to be confusing her own needs for care and attention with wanting to parent a child. She also came from a situation where to have children was the only way to achieve status and respect for a woman. In time, Chloe began to see some of her friends again and started to go out and enjoy herself. Her mother also recognised that Chloe needed extra support at this time. She spoke to her elder daughters and agreed to look after her grandchildren less often so that she could spend some time with Chloe that didn't involve babies and children.

Infertility

What does infertility mean?

So how do we define infertility? How long should it take to get pregnant? For the reasons highlighted above it is perhaps best to avoid using a time-scale as the sole factor to define fertility problems. It would be more relevant for you to consider with your GP your particular circumstances. In research studies often a cut-off time of attempting to conceive for a year or two is used to define infertility.

How common is infertility?

Research shows that about 14 per cent of women experience infertility: failure to conceive within two years. However, this statistic might be slightly misleading since around half of these women subsequently go on to have a child. Perhaps what is surprising, given the current climate of much media attention being given to the subject of fertility and fertility treatment, research has shown that only half of these women seek any medical advice. Interesting too is the fact that, of those who went on to conceive, just as many had not had any medical advice as those who had. Perhaps this is a further reason not to rush into seeking medical help. Other research has shown that the pattern of seeking help is changing very rapidly. In the past 25 years far more women and men are now seeking help for fertility-related issues.

What causes infertility?

A discussion of the causes of infertility is really beyond the scope of this book. A vast array of different aspects of the process of conception can be to blame: for women there may be problems with ovulation, a previous ectopic pregnancy or an infection may have damaged the fallopian tube. For men, a range of issues to do with the quantity and motility of the sperm may be relevant. These types of problems are termed primary fertility problems. However, it is interesting to highlight that some of the reasons for not conceiving are not simply a 'technical' fault of the reproductive system or primary infertility, some of the reasons stem from a complicated mixture of physical and psychological reasons. These problems are termed secondary infertility.

Primary problems lend themselves to investigation but sometimes no physical problems can be identified and a sizeable group of people have what is termed 'unexplained' infertility. Clearly, the psychological costs of such a diagnosis are high. Sometimes the causes of infertility can be directly due to other problems, illnesses or drug treatments. Sometimes you will have been directly informed of these risks, e.g. that a particular type of medication causes impotence. However, other problems may be hidden: a previous history of anorexia nervosa can lead to fertility problems but if the eating problems were never recognised in the past, then this reason may not be apparent. Other more subtle influences on fertility are drinking and smoking which are clearly factors that can be changed.

Often the inability to conceive is related to sexual difficulties. There are probably no problems relating to actual conception but the relationship is either not consummated or intercourse is rare. These clearly are problems of conception but the solutions are very different.

Ali and Maria's story

Ali and Maria came to see me for help with relationship problems. They had been married for nearly a year but the relationship did not appear to be consummated. Maria had been studying in England when she met Ali and had come from Greece to live permanently here when they married. Ali was Algerian and the couple communicated in English although it was not their first language. Communication was undoubtedly difficult and the couple seemed unable to make the other understand how they felt. Ali desperately wanted children and was sure that Maria did too. Consequently Ali was perplexed by their inability to have a full sexual relationship. Maria, however, appeared much more ambivalent about everything. In marrying Ali she had left her family and her home and had given up her studying to work in a restaurant. Ali ran the restaurant and organised when Maria would be working. When Ali was working, she mostly sat at home alone in their flat and had made few friends. She said she had planned to be a teacher and was not worried about when children came along since she was still very young.

Sadly, Ali and Maria's marriage did not survive these problems. Maria returned home to her mother for a holiday and failed to return. Ali began to look into having the marriage annulled.

The solutions to these types of 'fertility' problems are complicated and need a different type of assessment by someone specialising in sexual problems. There may be underlying issues such as childhood sexual abuse or intense anxiety concerning sexuality. Very often issues are to do with power and control within relationships. For Maria, avoiding sex meant avoiding children in a situation where she felt unable to articulate her own views and needs.

Christine and Kevin's story

Christine and Kevin had been happily married for five years and were in a secure position financially and both wanted to have a family. Christine said that both sets of parents were eagerly awaiting the announcement of a pregnancy. In fact, Christine's mother had tentatively asked her if there were 'any problems' and said that 'at 33 she shouldn't waste too much time'. Christine came for help because she had never managed to have intercourse with her husband. She said that they were both fully happy with their sexual relationship as it was but they did want to have children. Christine was also actively perusing fertility treatment through the private sector, as she didn't really feel her sexual difficulties were likely to change.

What help is available?

If you are desperate to be pregnant, are in your late thirties and have been trying for many months, then you may feel that you have 'no time to lose' in terms of investigating whether or not there is a problem. However, there are costs to entering the realms of testing. Any type of testing brings with it the risk of 'false positives', that is, a problem may be identified, for example, a man may be told he has a low sperm count, which may in fact not prove to be significant at all. However, being told that you have a 'low sperm count' may have powerful effects on your self-esteem, on your relationship, and particularly on your sexual relationship. Taking any form of testing turns the situation into a 'problem' and may exert unwanted pressure on your sexual relationship. These factors need to be balanced against the realities of your personal situation: your age and your medical history, for example.

Your GP is undoubtedly the best person to approach in the first instance. Although there is a vast array of services available privately, an initial contact with your GP should help you to identify whether you need to embark upon any further testing and intervention. Once the process is set in motion there is a wide array of treatments available depending on what the specific problems are.

Taking a different path

Many couples will decide that intervention isn't a path they wish to peruse. Often this is down to finances, where treatments are only available to them at a cost beyond their means. Many couples decide to move on and embrace a child-free life and enjoy the social and financial advantages of their position. Perhaps for some in this position they still remain hopeful that a baby might come along at some point. Some couples pursue fostering or adoption, perhaps taking on a very different family situation to the one they had imagined when they started their journey.

Martha and Ted's story

Martha had struggled with anorexia throughout her adult life. She couldn't remember a time when she had ever eaten freely and she had been treated as an inpatient numerous times. At 39 Martha looked more like a woman in her sixties. Her skin had aged dramatically, she remained very thin and slightly stooped – her body clearly displayed the effects of a lifetime of starvation. However, at 35 Martha's life had taken a massive leap forward when she had met Ted who was 50 and divorced. Within a year they married. Martha had never given up the hope of having a baby and at 42, after seven years of trying, she finally fell pregnant and successfully delivered a son.

The emotional impact of fertility problems and treatments

Again, there isn't room here to cover the vast array of treatments and procedures that are involved in assisted conception. However, it is clear that the emotional costs of fertility problems can be significant. Those diagnosed with fertility problems are more likely to be diagnosed as depressed; to have anxiety problems; to report relationship problems and specifically higher levels of difficulty with their sexual relationship. The treatments themselves can exert extreme physical and psychological pressures and as many as two-thirds of procedures do not result in a baby. For some couples, despite massive intervention at great personal and financial cost, a baby is never achieved.

Sadly, fertility issues are also not uncommon for those who already have a child. The sense of loss and disappointment and personal failure can be just as intense for the individual or couple even though they already have a child.

India and Chris's story

India had her first baby at 36 with IVF ten years after they first started trying for a child. Grace brought so much happiness, and with India aware of her age, they tried again quite quickly for another child and conceived twins. Sadly the babies were lost before the end of the first trimester. India spent a couple of years getting over this loss while trying to carry on with life as normal for the sake of Grace. Chris was 'desperate' that they should have a sibling for Grace and so at 42 India again became pregnant. She was referred for help with depression as she found herself crying 'for no reason' and couldn't understand why. In therapy it was extremely hard for India to admit that in many ways she regretted getting pregnant again. She said she had now had 'more cycles of IVF than she could remember' which had mainly been paid for by her parents and hence she felt 'this responsibility to give them grandchildren for their investment'. She felt that the treatment had aged her, she had missed out on time with Grace and she felt angry about having lost the twins. Grace was now at school and she felt another baby would mean 'going back to the beginning again'. Having opened up this discussion India began to talk to Chris who also admitted he had some reservations about having another child, particularly the financial implications. Chris was approaching 50 and felt his future earning potential was uncertain. Towards the end of the pregnancy, however, they both had much more positive feelings about their future. They had been helped particularly by Grace's enthusiasm about having a baby brother.

Who can help?

Where you are having problems with conceiving or if you have any issues to do with timing your pregnancy (for example, following a miscarriage), then your GP is the best person to contact initially. Your GP can discuss your own unique circumstances with you and help you decide first of all whether or not there is a problem. Your GP will also be able to advise you on what services are available locally on the NHS, as these do vary between areas. If you want to, or have to, approach the private sector, then your doctor may also have past experience of particular services and may be able to recommend a particular clinic.

If you feel you might have problems getting pregnant due to more complicated emotional or sexual problems then you will need to discuss the nature of these difficulties with the GP who may be able to refer you to a psychosexual counsellor or clinic, to a relationship therapist or to a general mental health specialist such as a clinical psychologist. The organisation Relate specialises in relationship and psychosexual counselling but they do charge a fee. The number of your local branch will be in the phone book or you can access more information via their website (see the list of addresses on p. 181).

Discussion points

1. What are the implications for you as a couple in becoming a family: personal, emotional, financial, career choices?
2. Timing: when would you like to start trying to conceive? You may wish to discuss what you would do if it doesn't all go to plan.
3. How long do you imagine it might take to get pregnant? How would you feel as a couple if it took one month, ten months, or three years?

3

The stages of pregnancy

Introduction

Mostly couples like to keep the news of their pregnancy to themselves, or a select few, for the first few weeks, hoping to have some time to adjust to their new situation before having to communicate it to others. The wish is often therefore to just 'carry on as normal'. However, many women find themselves unprepared for the intense physical and emotional changes of the early days of pregnancy. Only a minority of women 'don't feel any different'; a significant number will feel exhausted, at times nauseous, possibly vomiting. Many are upset easily, tearful, anxious or irritable and generally 'not themselves'. Pregnancy for every woman is different and every pregnancy is unique. Even if you have been through it all before, this doesn't necessarily make a subsequent pregnancy any easier or any more predictable. For the father-to-be, there are not the intense biological signals to remind him of the baby's existence, so life may seem just the same as ever. It can, therefore, be difficult for him to understand what his partner is going through. He may feel unsympathetic to a partner who was rushing to get pregnant and who now is losing their temper at every opportunity. Alternatively, now you are pregnant, you may feel terrified by the pregnancy and find it difficult to understand how your partner is carrying on as if nothing has changed. For both parents-to-be it may be a time of intense anxiety and self-doubt about becoming a parent. The news may highlight difficulties in the relationship, particularly where there may have been thoughts of, or actual separation, in the past.

As the pregnancy progresses, most women move into a mid-phase, which is often characterised by feeling well, often exceptionally so:

mothers are often described as 'blooming'. Whether this is primarily a physical change is not clear, but feeling well does allow time for a shift in focus where parents can start preparing for the baby. This might mean practical things like shopping for prams but it may also allow time for pondering more complex emotional changes: how will I cope with a tiny baby? What will it be like having another person within our relationship: how will three work? However, having accepted that you are pregnant, with birth still a way off it can be possible to 'get on with things' almost as you did before.

Often there will be a third phase, where, as the pregnancy starts to draw to an end you may start to feel more tired. Sleep often declines. This can be explained by increasing physical discomfort but this is also a time for a return of fears and anxieties that may have subsided mid-pregnancy. Often fears focus on labour and birth, or, coping with the baby. Many fathers may not have felt these anxieties early in the pregnancy and may have been in the role of reassuring their partner. The obvious imminence of the birth may be the first point at which fathers-to-be recognise that their life is to change irrevocably too!

This chapter will look at the feelings, emotions and events of pregnancy and how these may change over the course of 40 weeks. It will also consider the changing roles for the mother-to-be and father-to-be. For some women pregnancy is a very difficult and unhappy time. They may have been depressed before becoming pregnant; they may be struggling with an eating disorder or unhappy in their relationship. We all enter pregnancy from a unique place. The next chapter will move on to consider the experience of significant emotional problems in pregnancy.

The first few weeks: fears and acceptance

Will I feel like this for the whole nine months?

Pregnancy consists of three trimesters that are each about 13 weeks long and represent significant stages of the development of the baby. However, it is also possible to think about pregnancy as having three psychological phases, roughly overlapping with trimesters. The early weeks tend to focus on coming to terms with being pregnant and the fears and anxieties that may arise, coupled with the physical changes that can be surprisingly debilitating. Mid-pregnancy can be a more task-focused time as women feel better physically, time is spent in making preparations and plans for the baby. Towards the end of pregnancy fears, especially about labour, resurface and physical discomfort increases for many, as does a sense of wanting the pregnancy to end.

Not all women will experience these phases, one after another, but the issues raised are common to many pregnancies. The emotional journey through pregnancy can be looked at through the three stages outlined above.

'I just don't believe it': accepting the reality of the pregnancy

The early weeks of pregnancy can be awful, they can be exciting and feelings can change from one moment to the next. You may have been euphoric on discovering that you were pregnant, you might have been uncertain or you might have felt devastated. For most couples there is some ambivalence about what is happening, even in a pregnancy that was longed for. Very often the initial reaction to the discovery that you are pregnant may be surprising and disappointing. Once you are pregnant, everything can seem different. It is easy to be 100 per cent certain that you want a baby when you are trying to conceive but once you are pregnant, this certainty may be replaced by many fears. If your thoughts have been focused on getting pregnant, it may be only now that you are starting to wonder about how you will cope with a tiny baby. If the pregnancy has come as a surprise, then the sense of being unprepared or that this baby is an unwanted intrusion can be intense.

'I just don't want to believe it'

It is not unusual, especially in the early weeks of pregnancy, for women to feel negative feelings towards the baby: to feel intruded upon, to feel that you don't want this baby inside you. Some women may at times wish that the baby would miscarry or convince themselves that there has been a mistake with the pregnancy test. These sorts of feelings are seldom mentioned because women may be horrified by them; they think they are a terrible person for having such thoughts and fear that others will consider them a 'bad' person. But these feelings are not uncommon and having these thoughts does not mean you are going to act on them or be a bad parent. For most women the pregnancy will continue and normally these feelings disappear and are replaced by a different range of feelings and experiences. Men too can experience a range of feelings on discovering they are to become a father. Their greater distance from the baby (i.e. the baby not being inside them) perhaps allows for a wider range of reactions. They can express their ambivalence by ending the relationship, by avoiding thinking about the baby or by avoiding you.

A very unfortunate outcome is where women miscarry before coming to terms with the pregnancy and are left with terrible feelings of guilt that maybe they lost the baby because they didn't want it enough.

Christopher and Abigail's story

Christopher had been depressed quite severely for three years when he came to see me. He felt he had the perfect life: a good job, two children and a loving wife and yet he was depressed. He did find managing the children incredibly difficult and he admitted that he felt he lost his temper over very minor incidents with the children. However, he tended to become silent and withdrawn, brooding over what had happened and his wife would become totally exasperated with him, saying she had three children to look after. In the course of therapy it became clear that Christopher was terrified of becoming an angry father like his father had been. His depression had been triggered by his wife having a miscarriage. When Abigail had told him she was pregnant, he had 'flown off the handle' declaring it to be too soon, too much to cope with and Abigail had been shocked and upset by his reaction. The baby had miscarried at about seven weeks and Christopher had been consumed with guilt that he 'hadn't loved the baby enough while it was alive'.

Some women may go on to decide that they really don't wish to continue with the pregnancy. It is really important to get help and support on making a decision to terminate a pregnancy. Try to confide in a friend, partner or family member depending on whom you feel will be supportive. You may find it helpful to approach your GP or a Pregnancy Advisory Service (see the list of addresses on p. 181). Many women have to go through considering termination before they can make the decision to continue with the pregnancy.

'I don't know how to be a mother': fears in early pregnancy

Perhaps the other side of the coin or perhaps closely related to feeling negative towards the baby is to feel terribly fearful in early pregnancy:

will the baby be OK because I drank before I knew I was pregnant? Am I going to put on lots of weight? How do you pick up a baby? Lots of thoughts and feelings may cause both parents-to-be to feel quite anxious early on in the pregnancy or perhaps throughout. There are obviously some activities that should be avoided or foods that should not be eaten (see *The Pregnancy Book* given to all new mothers) but mostly fears are simply that; fears, part of assimilating this new life event. Nowadays we are somewhat bombarded with information in pregnancy about what not to eat or how to lead our lives and sometimes this information can seem contradictory. This disparity can in itself generate anxiety, 'If the professionals don't know the answer, then how can I know what is best?'

Resolving fears involves a number of factors: trying to understand the nature of these fears; getting more information where possible; making changes where necessary but mostly just allowing yourself time to come to terms with your new situation. Of course, fears won't necessarily go away completely, especially if you have a tendency to worry. There are many feelings that are common to this stage of pregnancy and some of them are explored below.

'I'm frightened that the baby won't be "normal"'

For very many women and their partners there are clearly fears about the health and development of the baby, especially early on in the pregnancy. This is extremely common and not just confined to first pregnancies. For a small percentage of women these fears are generated by a history of gynaecological or obstetric problems. Clearly if you have miscarried previously or had problems getting pregnant, then the degree of risk involved may become magnified in your mind. But for most these fears tend to be far greater than the actual risk.

Pregnancy in the twenty-first century is perceived to be a far less risky business than it was for previous generations. Alongside this fact we are given much information on how to have a healthy pregnancy: taking folic acid, cutting down on alcohol, and so on. Therefore, when something goes wrong it is not unusual for women to believe that *they* must have done something wrong. The reality is that the rate of miscarriage is now fairly constant and pregnancy loss or foetal abnormalities are rarely related to the actions of the mother (unless you are a drug user or a heavy drinker).

For most of us, pregnancy progresses without any problems but nevertheless if we have transgressed the 'rules', it may cause a great deal of guilt and hence fears that the baby may have been damaged in some way. For some there is even guilt about continuing a sexual relationship during the pregnancy (especially if there is any history of miscarriage). Pregnancy may awaken fears and guilt about previous behaviour such as termination of pregnancy or previous sexual partners. 'Perhaps I was damaged in some way by the termination', or 'caught some sort of infection' or 'my drinking will cause the baby to be malformed'. The problem with guilt is that it can get in the way of changing behaviour. It is very important to cut down or stop drinking and especially smoking in pregnancy. Guilt can make you defeatist, 'It's too late now, I've been smoking right through the first six weeks.'

For most women these fears will diminish as the pregnancy progresses safely and the first 'contacts' are made with the baby: seeing the baby on an ultrasound scan, hearing the baby's heartbeat and beginning to feel the baby move. It is not unusual for someone who might describe themselves as a 'worrier' for these feelings to continue throughout the pregnancy and some degree of anxiety is perfectly normal. For women who have had a late miscarriage or lost a baby at birth, it is not unusual for these fears to be very active throughout the pregnancy or until they have reached a self-defined marker: 'I'll feel alright once I get past 32 weeks or once the baby has been born.'

'I'm just not the "earth mother" type'

There are clearly fears for most prospective parents about how to be a parent. It is very hard for some to get beyond the belief that parenting is something instinctive not something learned: you either have it or you don't; some women are naturally maternal and some men 'know instinctively' how to be a father. Clearly some people seem to find it easier than others to care for a child but everyone struggles at times. Many women and their partners find it takes time to feel any attachment to, or love for, the baby. But attachment almost always occurs partly through getting to know the baby.

We all have the ability to learn and change and an enormous amount of learning takes place in those early days after the baby arrives: learning to change a nappy before the baby arrives isn't really necessary because after a week with a newborn you will have had plenty of practice. The baby himself will help you to learn as you grow to know him and understand his needs. Babies have evolved ways of getting you to feed them (crying) and getting you to look after them (making eye contact with you, responding to your voice and quite quickly smiling at you).

Other experiences, such as being around other new parents can be amazingly supportive in learning to be a parent. That's not because they know how to do it but partly because you can feel reassured that everyone else is learning too. You will see that not all babies are the same, need the same things or behave in the same way. Therefore, there is no blueprint of the 'right' way to do it. Hopefully it will be a time when you feel able to make mistakes and try things out. Donald Winnicott, an influential psychoanalyst and paediatrician, talked about the importance of new mothers being left alone with their baby to find their own natural way with the baby, and that too much interference from professionals and family can be unhelpful (Winnicott, 1988).

So why do some people find it easier than others? It is likely that if you had a very poor relationship with your own mother or father that this may play a part in the sort of parent that you become. That is not to say that you will be a 'bad' parent or 'do it just as they did' but if you have not felt loved and cared for yourself, then you may find having children brings a range of responses and feelings. Having to look after a demanding and needy baby may reawaken feelings of neediness in yourself. In fact, at times all parents will think, 'Well, what about me?' What seems to be crucial therefore is making sure that you have enough care and support *now* to help you give care and love to your baby. Research clearly shows that post-natal problems are less likely where a mother feels loved and cared for and supported. It is perhaps central to becoming a parent to recognise your own experience of being a child and how that plays a role in your self as a parent.

Jasmine's story

Jasmine had grown up in care and had her own baby when she was 17. When she first came to see me she was sure that her depression would resolve if she could have a breast enlargement operation. She hated the way she looked but believed she would be happier if she was more attractive. In time she began to recognise that she didn't really feel grown up since her own parenting had been so inadequate. Her mother had repeatedly placed her in care when she was small and eventually as a teenager the situation had become permanent and she had had a number of foster families. At 16 she was on her own: she had a baby without giving it much thought but it had made her feel as needy as a baby herself. To Jasmine the breast operation was simply about making herself look more attractive but it seemed also to represent changing herself on the outside to look like an adult woman, which she certainly did not feel on the inside. Jasmine borrowed money and saved up until she could have the operation, which did make her feel better – for a while.

'I'm terrified of getting fat (and stretch marks and varicose veins...)'

For many women there are intense fears about their changing body shape and the toll that pregnancy is going to exert over their body. Clearly one has to accept weight gain, an expanding stomach and breasts, and possibly permanent changes such as stretch marks and varicose veins. For the growth of the baby in pregnancy, healthy or 'normal' eating is important. But what is 'normal' and what exactly does 'healthy' mean? Mostly women are advised not to change or increase their diet (we are now discouraged from 'eating for two') but this assumes that you were eating reasonably well before you became pregnant. Research into women's eating behaviour, however, shows that a very large number of young women nowadays restrict their eating. Very many women control their eating very carefully; many do not eat proper regular meals and snack or binge and then miss meals to compensate. Therefore pregnancy might be the first time since you were a child that you have allowed yourself to eat freely.

Allowing yourself to lessen the control over your eating can feel very frightening. Many women hold (erroneous) beliefs that their popularity, confidence and abilities are linked to their weight and how they look. Therefore, becoming bigger will be very frightening. I cannot count how many times I have been met in therapy with the belief that the *only* way someone could be more successful/popular/attractive is by losing weight. Pregnancy therefore challenges these beliefs for some women.

Alternatively, 'losing control' may come as a great relief. It may provide a time of respite from the endless self-denial of dieting. It may offer the opportunity to relearn something about your appetite and what happens to you when you eat certain forbidden foods. Alicia, with whom I worked during one of her many inpatient admissions for anorexia, said that the only time she had ever enjoyed eating had been when she was pregnant as she could imagine that everything she ate went straight into the baby.

For some the fear of weight gain may be grounded, in that many women who are obese date their weight gain to starting a family. Nature has devised women's bodies so that they store fat in order to be prepared for breast-feeding. Many women find that they put on a great deal of weight in pregnancy and therefore general advice tends to advocate control over eating. Clearly, advice needs to be tailored to individual women's situations. If you continue to work to the end of your pregnancy in a physically demanding job, then it is very important to listen to what your body is telling you and eat if you are hungry. If you stop work early and find yourself around the home with time on your hands you may find yourself snacking through boredom. For the majority of women the fears are about loosening control over something that they have tried to keep a tight grip on ever since puberty. (See also the later section on eating disorders in pregnancy.)

'I don't think our relationship can cope with a baby'

It really is hard for any couple to imagine the impact that a child will have on their relationship. It is fair to say, as was touched on in the last chapter, that relationships change and probably will be strained in ways that they haven't been before. It's probably realistic to have some anxieties in this area but most relationships do learn to adapt and change.

During pregnancy some women fear their changing shape may affect their attractiveness to their partner, particularly that their partner may no longer find them sexually attractive. This can be more acute in the early stages of pregnancy, before the distinctive curves of pregnancy have developed, when a woman may feel that she looks 'fat' rather than pregnant. For fathers-to-be there may be issues about their partners changing shape but these are perhaps less common than concerns about changes in their sexual relationship. There is no medical or physical reason why your sexual relationship should not continue as before (unless you have received medical advice to the contrary). However, your or your partner's feelings about sex may change throughout the pregnancy. Some women feel unattractive as they change shape during pregnancy and if this is combined with feeling tired and unwell in early pregnancy, then this can severely disrupt a sexual relationship. This may be quite perplexing for a partner whose sexual feelings remains unchanged or if they in fact find their partner more attractive when pregnant. For some women too sexual feelings increase in pregnancy and some couples may find that their sexual relationship becomes better.

Sandra and Steve's story

Sandra had experienced bleeding during the early weeks of both of her pregnancies but went on to have two healthy babies. However, after the bleeding in her second pregnancy she stopped having intercourse with Steve, her husband. Steve didn't question Sandra about this, as he knew she was worried about the safety of the baby. However, a couple of months after the safe arrival of their daughter Steve began to wonder how he should approach the subject with Sandra. When they did eventually discuss it, in the middle of an argument, it became clear that Sandra's reluctance to have sex had had nothing to do with the safety of the baby and was all to do with being convinced that Steve didn't fancy her any more and must be attracted to someone else as he no longer seemed interested in sex with her.

When will these fears go away?

It is perfectly normal to have a number of fears and concerns in pregnancy especially early on. For most women these will subside as the pregnancy progresses and 'being pregnant' becomes part of your identity. However, if fears are too persistent or overwhelming, then they can affect your ability to get on with everyday life. This might be a time to look a little more closely at what is generating these problems either through discussion with a partner or friend or perhaps by seeking help from a professional. It may be that a discussion with a GP or midwife will provide information to challenge these fears or through discussion other issues may emerge.

It is important to learn to deal with fears, as they will carry on after the baby is born. As your baby grows and develops, you will still be full of questions about how he is doing. Should he be sitting up yet? Is his weight right? Is he saying enough? So finding a way of managing your fears is important.

'I've just got the job I want and now I'm pregnant': pregnancy as a life event

Pregnancy doesn't happen in a vacuum. As was discussed in the last chapter few of us are able to 'perfectly time' our conception. We all start pregnancy from a different place in our lives: at a certain point in our career, in or not in a relationship (or not sure), happy or miserable. These life factors will play a role in how we deal with the pregnancy. Psychological research has shown that our emotional health is affected by the number of *life events* that we are experiencing at any one time. This isn't just referring to negative events: so if you discover that you are pregnant, decide you would really like to marry before the baby is born and think that you should move out of your flat, then you may find yourself not enjoying or able to cope with these events that you may have always longed for.

The pregnancy therefore arrives into a context and its meaning is affected by the other events that are going on in your life. If you are desperately trying for a promotion at work, then even a wanted pregnancy can seem 'ill-timed' or 'in the way'. If you are a woman who is not working, then even an unplanned pregnancy may give a new focus to your life. For an unemployed dad-to-be pregnancy could be seen as a further burden in an already difficult situation or it could prove a new, motivating factor in the search for work. For increasing numbers of men it might lead to a complete life change in terms of deciding to become the main caretaker for the baby.

Feeling depressed, irritable or fearful in early pregnancy may have as much to do with the other events in our lives as they do with hormones. It may be that the pregnancy brings into focus a number of life issues: do I want to stay in this relationship? Can I carry on with this stressful job? The problem with attributing everything to 'the pregnancy' or 'my hormones' is that it can contribute to avoiding decisions and choices that will need to be made. Pregnancy does give some time to work on some of these life issues but only if they are viewed as problems external to the pregnancy that can be solved. Pregnancy, like other significant life events, makes us focus on how we are managing our life and whether we can cope with new responsibilities on top of the ones we already have or whether some things are going to have to change.

'Our baby was a "miracle" so I must be pleased'

It is not unusual for a couple who were desperate to have a baby, perhaps having fertility treatment to achieve it, to have mixed feelings about the pregnancy. Everyone is entitled to feel uncertain about having a baby. I have worked with many women who, having had assisted conception, find it terribly difficult, almost shameful to admit that they have felt anything other than total joy about their pregnancy. India and Chris, who were discussed in the last chapter, struggled with a wide range of feelings during their pregnancies especially the last. India had a deep sense of loss for the twins that had died and felt that she would never really get over the loss. She felt her current pregnancy to be ill-timed and she worried about having the energy to care for the new baby. However, to the outside world she tried to retain an image of serenity as she felt otherwise people would think her selfish and ungrateful for the child that she did have.

It is important for all parents-to-be to be able to feel miserable, scared and confused at times about what is happening. People around you are probably going to assume that you are nothing other than happy about the pregnancy, so it may be important to share these feelings with your partner or with a good friend. It becomes particularly important after the baby is born to be able to share your uncertainties and difficulties so now might be a good time to start practising.

'I've done it all before so I must know what I'm doing!'

As has been said previously, every pregnancy is different and just because you have been through it all before does not mean that you will sail through this time, or feel uncertain or ambivalent about the pregnancy. Second, third or even a fourth time round, a number of issues can make pregnancy difficult. Perhaps the pregnancy was unplanned or just seems to be going too quickly. You may find yourself so preoccupied with your other children and responsibilities that you have hardly a moment to think about and plan for this baby. You may need to make particular efforts throughout the pregnancy to make sure that you get enough time for yourself and to think about the new baby.

So, for both parents there can be much anxiety and uncertainty in early pregnancy. How much you are able to think about these issues is clearly affected by how well generally you are feeling. This, as we have said, is often not the case.

Morning sickness

I felt like a piece of delicate china; one small knock and I would completely fall to pieces.

It was like the longest and worst hangover I ever had.

The initial anxieties of pregnancy can, however, be completely over-shadowed by the overwhelming and unpleasant symptoms known as *morning sickness*. The term 'morning' can be misleading as the symptoms often continue throughout the day. Morning sickness can, of course, start before you know you are pregnant, almost as soon as conception has occurred. It may be what alerts you to the fact that you have conceived. These early pregnancy symptoms can be quite distressing especially if you are still reeling from the discovery that you are pregnant. Where there are mixed feelings about the pregnancy and thoughts of possible termination, this can be intensely distressing as the sickness brings a constant reminder of the reality of the pregnancy.

The onset of morning sickness can be very sudden. It is not unusual to go to bed wondering why you don't feel any different yet and to wake up feeling like you've been hit by a bus. All manner of symptoms, physical and emotional, can occur in early pregnancy and are explained by the umbrella term 'morning sickness'. The list below features a range of experiences women report:

- Tiredness/exhaustion: the tiredness of early pregnancy can be worse than the sleepless nights after the baby is born. Women may find themselves wanting to sleep much longer or more often than usual and yet sleeping may have little impact on the feelings of tiredness and lethargy. It's not unusual to spend a whole day in bed and still feel tired! This can be very disabling and the early weeks of pregnancy can seem unending. You may begin to worry: how will I cope with a baby if I can't cope with feeling tired now? Fortunately this malaise does lift as the pregnancy progresses.
- Nausea and vomiting: along with tiredness, the persistent sickness that some women experience can be the most debilitating part of pregnancy. It can affect all aspects of your life, making carrying on with everyday life almost impossible. Despite its debilitating effects it is only in extreme circumstances that vomiting leads to medical intervention or hospitalisation. There is in fact little that can be done to stop vomiting in pregnancy and most women simply try to endure it and adapt their lives as much as possible, hoping that the symptom will soon pass.
- Breast changes, feeling bloated and other menstrual-type symptoms.
- Strange tastes, going 'off' foods or cravings. Many women report a metallic taste in their mouths. Classically women reject certain foods or develop preoccupations with particular foods. There may be good adaptive reasons why women 'crave' certain foods, perhaps their bodies are identifying their nutritional needs. However, the preoccupation often with one item makes this seem unlikely. In extreme cases non-food items such as coal have been the object of cravings, which would be hard to explain in physiological terms.
- Headaches, general aches and pains.
- Tearfulness, angry outbursts, anxiety symptoms. How much these feelings are due to hormonal or physical changes is unclear but the issues highlighted earlier in combination with these physical changes make a powerful cocktail. Nevertheless at the time these feelings can be confusing for both parents-to-be especially in a planned and wanted pregnancy.

Do men get morning sickness too?

Although the physical symptoms highlighted above should be common only to women, it may be that partners too experience unpleasant thoughts and feelings in early pregnancy. The early pregnancy does impact far less on the father/partner and probably he is going to be less troubled now by worries about becoming a parent. However, some may find themselves anxious and confused.Where perhaps this is not understood as 'anxiety', this may result in physical symptoms in the partner. As we have said in relation to women we cannot be sure that all of the physical symptoms of morning sickness are generated hormonally, therefore, worries in the partner may lead to feelings of nausea, headaches and pains, and so on. More often than not, anxiety can lead to behavioural changes or what Psychologists might call 'acting out'. The news of a pregnancy may lead the partner to increase alcohol or drug use. He might stay out more, stay at work later or be more argumentative. Relationships are often delicately balanced in terms of who supports who and if a woman suddenly becomes less able to function because of morning sickness, then a partner may feel uncared for, put upon, frustrated. If the situation was such that the woman was more insistent on becoming pregnant, the partner may feel resentful that the woman has brought all these problems when the situation was fine as it was.

Partners often try to change their behaviour and attitudes when a woman becomes pregnant, especially where there is bad morning sickness or a history of pregnancy difficulties. The partner may start to do more of the domestic chores, he may avoid areas of conflict and try to adapt to how the woman is feeling. This can inevitably lead to tension: if you have done your best to tidy up or prepare a meal and your partner goes straight to bed without noticing, you may find yourself feeling resentful or frustrated. Often the partner finds himself in the role of confused bystander attempting to offer support but feeling totally perplexed by what is going on: 'You wanted to be pregnant and now you are, you're miserable the whole time.'

How to cope with morning sickness

There is no clear explanation for what causes morning sickness other than the obvious physiology of early pregnancy. However, nothing has been specifically indicated, such as an excess of a particular hormone, that would explain why some women sail through early pregnancy feeling no different and others are practically confined to bed for three months! Nor is their any interesting psychological research looking at whether the emotional aspects of pregnancy and the physical symptoms can be managed any differently. This leads us on to consider possible ways of managing morning sickness.

Information about morning sickness

What seems quite amazing is the fact that women do cope so well with morning sickness. Clearly if one were to feel like this without an explanation, then we would all be queuing at the doctor's surgery for treatment and probably absent from work. This doesn't seem to be the case. Generally, even with quite debilitating symptoms, women seem to carry on with their lives and don't demand specific help. An important factor therefore seems to be that we have a *reason* for our symptoms, which suggests that the more we are informed about what is happening to our bodies, the better able we are to cope. It is probably worthwhile at this time finding out what is happening to your body as it may help to put things into some sort of context. Your GP will probably give you some written information at your booking visit that will give diagrams and details of the development of the baby. All women should be given a copy of *The Pregnancy Book* by the Health Education Authority.

Once conception has occurred, an amazingly complex physiological process gets under way with remarkable speed. By 12 weeks your baby is fully formed, in that it has all its organs, muscles, limbs and bones, although it would not be 'viable' or able to live outside of the womb until at least 24 weeks. This is a staggering achievement for your body, and with such rapid development of the baby perhaps it is not surprising that we feel a little swept off our feet at times. When we consider the remarkable processes going on within the woman's body, it is perhaps more difficult to understand why some women feel nothing at all.

Lifestyle changes

It is certainly true that for most problems in life, whether physical or psychological, the more that we feel that we have some influence over them, the less we become victim to them, and the same thinking can be applied to morning sickness. Many women view morning sickness as a sign from their body that they need to change their lifestyle, perhaps change their diet, limit the range or type of activity they engage in, increase the amount of sleep/rest they are getting, limit their drinking,

and so on. This approach can of course prove unpopular if you have told
yourself that 'having a baby won't change my life' or 'I'm not going to
give up my interests just because I'm having a baby'. Perhaps it's important to remember that morning sickness doesn't last for ever and there
is no harm in doing it differently for a while. Getting more sleep,
avoiding where possible stressful situations, leaving aside troublesome
tasks until you feel better and changing your diet may all help. There
are books offering more specific advice but perhaps what is most
important is to respond to what your body is telling you: rest when
you are tired, eat when you feel hungry. As mentioned earlier, women
seem to be remarkably adaptive at dealing with these symptoms and
finding their own individual solutions.

Relaxation

Often during pregnancy women learn the skill of relaxation to cope in
labour but it may also help to cope with morning sickness. The reading
list on p. 188 includes some relaxation tapes, which can be purchased.
Simply follow the instructions on the tape. You may be able to borrow
tapes from your local library. You may also find that using your own selec-
tion of music is more relaxing. People dealing with a whole range of
unpleasant symptoms, such as chronic pain, find that learning the skill
of relaxation can significantly reduce their experience of pain. Partly this
can work by learning to focus on positive images and thoughts rather than
the distressing symptom, which can reduce their experience of pain.
Learning to relax certainly won't make the sickness and fatigue go away
but at the very least it may just encourage you to take ten minutes out
every day to put your feet up: after all, the weeks when sickness occurs are
crucial in the development of the baby.

'I still can't believe I'm pregnant': the increasing role of technology in our experience of pregnancy

If you 'feel your usual self' in early pregnancy, then it may be hard to
believe that you are pregnant and impossible to imagine that there is a
baby growing inside of you. However, in recent years technology increasingly plays a role in our understanding and experience of pregnancy. For
our mothers and grandmothers the first sight of the baby was at birth but
today almost all women have at least one ultrasound scan. Many women
are now offered a (nuchal) scan at 10–13 weeks pregnant to assess the risk of

Down's Syndrome or they may have an early scan to confirm the pregnancy itself. Nearly all women will have a scan at 20–24 weeks to assess the development of the baby.

The scan can be a magical moment for both mother-to-be and father-to-be as the baby can be viewed with remarkable clarity, its tiny movements are visible and its limbs and structures can be identified. This can be a highly emotional moment for the couple, who may feel they have 'become parents' in seeing their baby for the first time. There is evidence to show that the scan helps to make the baby seem more real to the parents but this doesn't actually influence the later relationship with the baby. Bonding with the baby is a more complicated process. Nevertheless, when asked in research, women said they would like more scans, as they feel they bring reassurance about the growth and well-being of the baby. As previously mentioned many women have anxieties about the development of the baby and scanning might seem an obvious way of reducing these but in fact a scan does not seem to reduce levels of anxiety except in a very temporary way. For further information on the psychology of ultrasound scans, see Clement *et al.* (1998). Overall, ultrasound scans seem to be a positive experience for parents-to-be.

Twin and multiple pregnancies

Discovering that you are having more than one baby can come as an enormous shock. Sometimes parents-to-be are aware of a family history of twins but even so the news can be quite overwhelming until you get used to it. Medically twin pregnancies are more complicated as usually the babies are born earlier and more intervention is common. However, your psychological adaptation does not necessarily need to be more negative although the likelihood of more medical complications can increase the psychological risks. After the babies are born, there may be a greater risk of them needing special care and you also have more than one new person to get to know! These factors can make a multiple pregnancy more complicated but clearly your expectations are going to be different: you will probably be more prepared for uncertainty and intervention concerning your delivery which may make the experience easier to come to terms with.

Today many multiple pregnancies are the result of fertility treatment and therefore may have been expected. The meaning here can be different too. You may be delighted with more than one baby if you have struggled for years with the prospect of no children or if this is your last attempt at assisted conception. Alternatively you may have agreed to the implementation of more than one egg with the very strong hope that this would produce just one baby and now feel overwhelmed by this news. There are now restrictions on the number of eggs that can be implanted for this reason.

Getting rid of bad habits: drinking and smoking issues

We probably all agree that in an ideal world pregnant women would avoid alcohol and never smoke or take any other form of non-prescribed drug. However, many women are not aware that they are pregnant until well into the first trimester, others may find it more difficult than they had imagined to change their habits. It is unhelpful when people are told in a matter-of-fact way to give up drinking or smoking as if it were as easy as changing your clothes. For many people making such changes is enormously difficult. It is important to make these changes, not just in pregnancy, therefore getting as much advice and support as possible is crucial. Below follows some general suggestions but it is always worth seeing if your GP can recommend any further agencies or individuals that can help.

How can I cut down on my drinking?

For some women discovering that they are pregnant will be enough motivation for them to stop drinking or cut it down to the occasional drink. For others though this will be more difficult especially where you 'don't feel any different' or your social life revolves around drinking. It may be that you need to apply some structure to dealing with the problem.

- *Getting started:* The best time to start is probably before you get pregnant but it may be more difficult to motivate yourself when the pregnancy is still a possibility. For others the pregnancy may occur in a less planned way and you may be a few weeks into the pregnancy before you decide to take this step. Some women are fortunate that the pregnancy itself leaves them turned off by the smell or taste of alcohol.
- *How much am I drinking now?* Take a look back over the last couple of weeks and see how many units of alcohol you are drinking per week. For an explanation of alcohol units, ask your GP for the Health Education Authority leaflet. Don't just guess, as most people tend to underestimate their intake, in particular, calling any size of glass of alcohol one unit.

- *What do I want to achieve?* It is important to establish what you want to achieve. There is some evidence that any amount of alcohol has an effect on the developing foetus, so stopping altogether would be the ideal. However, many women are looking at reducing their alcohol intake rather than complete abstinence. Decide on a specific goal, e.g. none or a drink on special occasions, a couple of drinks per week or one per day. If the gap between where you are now and where you want to get to is not large then it may just be a case of making your mind up to start. However, if your drinking is heavy, regular and feels out of control, then you may need to take a number of steps to achieve your ultimate goal. There is no recommended number of units of alcohol that it is safe to drink in pregnancy and, therefore, almost any number of units could be termed 'heavy' drinking in pregnancy. It is perhaps more relevant to focus on how much of a challenge it will be for you to reduce this to a minimum.
- *Keep a diary:* It is important to monitor your progress and particularly your setbacks so keeping a diary can prove enormously informative. The way you record the information and what you record are up to you. It is useful to record for each drink where you were (*just got home from work*), the reason for drinking or how you felt (*felt stressed/always have one when I get in*) and whether you might have done anything else (*got straight into the bath*). For diary sheets, see p. 185.
- *Set up a system of alternative rewards:* The main reason that we drink is that most find it a pleasurable activity, so we need to replace this with some alternative reward. Deciding upon what you find rewarding is a very personal thing. You might need to substitute a few drinks with a nice meal, or you may save the money and buy some jewellery or go for a massage. Try to reward yourself frequently particularly in the early stages. Saying you'll save all the money to buy something after the baby is born may not prove successful if you are going to a string of parties.
- *Activities incompatible with drinking:* Pubs tend to be filled with people drinking and smoking and this is the worst place to be if you want to stop drinking. Try to expand or change your social activities to avoid such situations as much as possible. Avoiding places and people can be a very helpful strategy initially while you set up new routines and habits. Try to do activities when seeing friends (see a film, go for a walk) rather than just 'going for a drink'.
- *Change your routine:* Often a percentage of one's alcohol intake is purely through habit. If you always go to the pub on a Sunday or have a drink when you get in from work, then try to arrange alternative activities,

make a phone call, listen to some music, start a relaxation programme. Try not to have alcohol in the house: well-stocked wine racks are not helpful.

- *Try to get your partner to give up too:* This can be enormously helpful in terms of increasing your motivation and in changing your lifestyle/ social life. Many pregnant women feel that they become the 'taxi' service while pregnant and breast-feeding and this can be the source of much resentment when these were shared social activities prior to the pregnancy.

- *Review your progress:* Keeping a diary can be amazingly informative. It should help you to identify some of the problems and hopefully clues to the solutions areas. What are the 'triggers' to your drinking, e.g. situations, events or emotions that lead you to drink? What were the alternatives? You may find that certain situations or feelings lead you to drink and if you are finding it difficult to make progress then it may be that some of these factors need further exploration. If you feel stressed after a day at work and must have a drink try to 'unpick' that situation: why are you feeling so stressed at work? What aspects of the situation can be changed? It may be that you go on to keep a diary to monitor other situations and begin to reward yourself for dealing with those differently.

- *Now I've got other problems:* The use of alcohol often masks other problems and this can be what makes it so difficult to stop. For instance, many people drink to give themselves confidence in social situations or to feel like 'one of the crowd'. Stopping drinking may not be the problem but gaining more confidence in social situations may be the issue. It may be that you discover that you need help with a set of issues unrelated to drinking.

- *Getting more help:* If you don't make any progress with stopping drinking within a couple of weeks, then it may be time to seek further help. In pregnancy there really is no time to waste, as every day is important to the development of the baby. Problem drinking is merely a symptom of other more complicated issues that need looking in to. Your GP is always the best place to start in that he or she should know which particular facilities are available locally.

A similar programme or structure can be used for giving up smoking. Again, see your GP for help and advice, as there may be facilities available locally to help you. There is an NHS 'quitline' with help for giving up smoking in pregnancy and the number is in the list of addresses on p. 181.

Miscarriage

Most pregnancies that miscarry are lost in the first trimester. Some women experience a slight bleeding during these first few weeks and the pregnancy continues without any problem. For others it signals the end of the pregnancy. Some women unfortunately discover that they have miscarried when they go for a first scan. The baby has died but there have yet to be any signs of the loss. Most parents will not know exactly why the miscarriage has occurred and only if you have three miscarriages in a row is it considered medically necessary to investigate why it happened.

The emotional experience of miscarriage is more complicated. Many parents-to-be are devastated by their loss and take many months to recover. Often recovery is hampered by guilt about having in some way caused the miscarriage or fears about what this means. Is there something wrong with me? Will I ever conceive again?

Michelle's story

Michelle was referred for help with depression. She had miscarried two pregnancies both in the second trimester. In order to reassure her the doctors had told her that it was 'right' that nature had taken its course since her second baby had been very small for his gestational age and might have been born with a variety of problems. Rather than reassuring Michelle, this had left her with the feeling that she had produced a 'monster' and she was terrified of becoming pregnant again although she desperately wanted to try for a child.

In time, as Michelle's grief passed, she was able to channel some of her energies into preparing herself for another pregnancy: getting fit, eating well and trying to challenge an underlying sense of not being good enough that stemmed back to her own childhood.

Miscarriage is also very common for women who have already had children and the emotional effects can be just as acute even if you already have children. Feelings of grief can be intense whenever a pregnancy is lost. For many women who already have children, the lost pregnancy might be seen as the 'last chance'. It may signal a time for acceptance that your family is complete, particularly where a person feels they are getting too old to try again or their children are getting older and there would be too much of an age gap. This sense of loss may be particularly acute where the child was conceived through assisted conception and the chances of another attempt at getting pregnant have huge personal and financial implications with the prospect of conception low.

Another pregnancy?

Many people find it difficult to react to someone who has lost a baby and try to minimise the event: 'Well, don't worry, you can try again' or 'at least you know you can get pregnant'. These often well-intentioned comments can be very upsetting when someone is still coming to terms with their loss. They were expecting to have a baby on a particular date and would have begun to plan towards that event. One of the first things people ask is 'When is it due?' Although the pregnancy may have only lasted a couple of weeks, there may be much grief to follow in the future such as the date the baby was expected. Some women/couples feel ready to contemplate another pregnancy straightaway. However, not everyone will want to have another pregnancy or be ready to think about it until some time later.

Where a woman does go ahead after a miscarriage and have another pregnancy, this can be an emotionally difficult time. Often they experience anxiety or depression related both to fears about the pregnancy and feelings of loss for the miscarried pregnancy. Some writers have talked of an 'absence of involvement' whereby the mother is unwilling to invest emotionally in the pregnancy because of fears of further loss and pain. There is no amount of time that will be the 'right time' to embark upon another pregnancy since recovery is such an individual process. What is important is to recognise that you might feel anxious or detached in the next pregnancy. Therefore the right time is when you feel ready to face this.

In Chapter 5 stillbirth and neonatal loss will be discussed. This generally refers to a baby lost after 20/24 weeks and up to one month old.

Nikki's story

Nikki came to see me for help with depression following five miscarried pregnancies. She had spent most of her thirties either pregnant, trying to get pregnant or waiting to try and get pregnant again. While waiting to see me she had conceived again and had immediately been seen by the specialist services that were to monitor her pregnancy and administer drugs to try to maintain the pregnancy through the first trimester. Nikki herself felt totally unable to feel anything positive about the pregnancy and rather reluctantly admitted that she had not wanted to take the drugs she was prescribed because of the potential risks to her own health. However, so sure were her doctors that she would do anything to maintain the pregnancy they had failed to fully check out her willingness to take the drug. Understandably, despite being pregnant, she could feel nothing other than terribly depressed and confused about her feelings towards the pregnancy. She was unwilling to feel anything positive because of the enormous risk of another loss and she was still overwhelmed with the grief of her previous losses. Sadly, the pregnancy miscarried before 12 weeks. Also part of her grief was an acceptance that this was to be the last attempt. Her partner had distanced himself from the situation having decided some time ago that they should not try again.

A time for change

The first few weeks of pregnancy may therefore have been a longer journey than you had imagined. You may have been struggling with changing your lifestyle: perhaps trying to stop smoking or drinking. Sickness may have led you to telling lots of people about your pregnancy before you had planned to. You may have felt unable to do some of your usual activities and found yourself needing more sleep. Partners may have been taken aback by the changes in you and have had to take over certain tasks at home. Your life may be changing far more quickly than you had predicted. For both of you there may have been many surprises in terms of how you have reacted emotionally.

The practice of not announcing your pregnancy until a number of weeks have elapsed probably has much to do with the complicated emotional situation of the first couple of months. It is perfectly normal to be overwhelmed by the discovery of being pregnant, after all until this point the life changes are hypothetical but now the situation has changed irreversibly: even if you were to decide not to continue with the pregnancy or you miscarry you can never return to the previous situation.

The mid-pregnancy: making plans

The second trimester of pregnancy starts at 13 weeks. The baby now concentrates on growing in size and its organs continue to mature.

During this trimester the baby's movements are first felt. You may feel a tiny flutter early on or your first sign may be a more discernible kick! As the baby grows in size, your partner may be able to feel these movements too.

The middle months of pregnancy may be a very different time psychologically from the experiences we have talked about in early pregnancy. Generally women feel healthier, their morning sickness having subsided and usually the pregnancy has been 'accepted', in that the woman feels more able to get on with everyday life, not as before, but in the new identity of *pregnant woman*. Obviously every pregnancy is unique and if you don't start to feel better, this isn't a sign of something being 'wrong' with the pregnancy. There may be many reasons for this: if you already have a toddler to look after it may be difficult to recover from the extra demands that the pregnancy is placing on your resources – both physical and psychological. It may be that your relationship is still adapting to the prospect of the baby or for a variety of reasons you may simply not be enjoying pregnancy.

Feeling better

Beginning to feel better physically will clearly contribute to the feeling of having entered a new stage of the pregnancy. Therefore, if we think of there being a 'psychological' mid-phase of pregnancy, this will coincide with beginning to feel better physically and this could occur anywhere from 12 to 20 weeks. Morning sickness often begins abruptly but usually trails off, with a gradual reduction in the nausea and a feeling that you are less tired and more able to carry out your life tasks as you did before. For some women this can actually move into a stage of feeling better than they have ever done. Pregnant women are often described as 'blooming' at this time. It can be a time of feeling physically and emotionally very good. How much of this shift is due to physical changes and how much is due to the emotional fact of having accepted the pregnancy is not clear.

The mid-pregnancy can seem quite a relaxed time: you have adjusted to the pregnancy but the arrival of the baby is still some way off. The baby can still be carried around easily and for most women the pregnancy does not limit their activities. At this point the baby itself is 'safe' and reasonably undemanding – perhaps the odd kick to let you know he is there. So 'living with the baby' may become a very positive experience: the baby can 'come to life' in terms of its intermittent movements, its heartbeat can be heard at an ante-natal visit and its features can be now made out in a scan. At the same time, it can be 'forgotten' about if the mother wants to get on with her work or things that made up her life before she was pregnant. This could be termed a time of compromise between mother and baby before the time when, after birth the needs of the baby seem to dominate your every waking moment! You have adjusted to being the mother of a baby that is contained within you.

'But how many babygros do I need?'

In the long journey of pregnancy nature therefore provides us with some welcome time and space for preparing for the arrival of the baby, both practically and emotionally. Not every family is the same but there are some issues that are common to many women and couples at this stage.

On a practical level, one has to make a space for the baby and begin to think about what he might need in those early weeks. This is really as much a psychological task as a practical one in that it involves imagining having this new person in your home and dependent on you for his needs. A whole new area of knowledge needs to be acquired such as how to attach the baby's seat to the car or how to place a baby in a cot to sleep. In fact, most of these things don't really make sense until the baby arrives. It is easy for this planning in itself to become a source of stress and anxiety. Many parents are bamboozled by the vast array of goods, intensively marketed, that lead us to believe that we *must* acquire them otherwise our baby will not be safe or will not be 'stimulated'. Finding the money to pay for everything can be a source of stress: parents may feel cheated if right from the start they cannot get 'the best' for their baby. Few of the things that we buy for babies are really essential. Often hospitals or midwives provide lists of 'essentials' and attending ante-natal classes or talking to other new mothers is helpful.

These practical tasks – decorating a room or buying vests – can help to make the baby seem more real in your life and may help you to think about how your life will change after his arrival. It can also help you to feel that you are doing something constructive, which can be a relief if you have a lot of fears that don't seem to have answers at the moment.

What do the contractions feel like? Learning new skills for pregnancy and birth

Lots of thoughts may be coming now about the labour and the birth and how best to prepare for this and how to care for a new baby. One aspect of this might be enrolling in ante-natal or parenting classes, which will usually begin in the third trimester. Chapter 5 will look at labour and birth in more detail but it is never too early to start researching what types of classes are available locally. Your midwife or GP should be able to help with this. (See also the 'Who can help?' section on p. 67.) There is enormous variation in what classes are offered. Most NHS maternity services will offer classes run by midwives and health visitors. There are also organisations such as the National Childbirth Trust that run classes. You may be able where time, finances and availability allow, to attend more than one type.

Overall, it is probably not worth worrying too much about the content of the classes as the chance of being with other parents-to-be and sharing your experiences of pregnancy is just as useful as the factual information given. If fathers attend groups too, this can really help a mother to feel supported and can help the father to feel more involved, more informed and less anxious. If the group can continue to meet after the babies are born, then this will offer great support in those early months with the baby. It may be hard in pregnancy to believe that you want to keep meeting with a group of 'strangers' but the shared experience of having a new baby can be very important especially if all your friends are at work during the week.

As well as preparing for labour, it may also be a time for beginning to consider what changes you are to face as a couple: how will your life be different? It really can be difficult to imagine what it will be like when the baby arrives but this should not discourage you from beginning the discussion. Prospective parents tend to worry about the *tasks* of caring for a baby, for example, how often should I change a nappy? Most people haven't changed a nappy before having a baby and it can seem complicated before you've tried but, rest assured by the end of first few days, you will feel like an expert after so much practice! Parents don't go to health visitors in the weeks after birth saying 'I still can't change a nappy!' They are much more likely to present with problems about *who* is changing the nappies. Consequently it does no harm to begin now to think about how things are going to be different after the baby is born. What aspects of your life now do you particularly value and what do you feel you could give up? How flexible can your partner be in terms of time commitments? Who else is around to help?

So the journey to becoming a competent parent isn't fully explained by the practical tasks that have to be mastered. However difficult labour might be, it does have a finite point whereas balancing your own needs versus meeting those of your offspring is a task that continues throughout childhood.

Can I go part-time? The decisions regarding work

The majority of women are probably working when they have their first pregnancy. For many it is in this stage of pregnancy that ideas begin to formulate about their work situation. Some women will just about be able to see far enough forward to decide roughly when they want to start maternity leave. Others will have clear ideas about what they want to do work-wise over the course of the next few years.

In the last chapter a number of issues were discussed in terms of women and children and work generally but now may be a time to consider your own personal situation and feelings and what is right for you. It is important to sit down with your partner and for both of you to discuss your views and expectations about what will happen after the baby arrives (see 'Discussion points' on p. 67). Although you might not know what you want to do about returning to work you can still discuss what role you might play while at home. You will find that whatever decision you make, you will have to justify it to other people: employers, friends, grandparents, and so on.

It probably doesn't matter how formed your ideas are as long as they are not too rigidly held. You may be lucky and 'do it to plan' but it's hard to imagine that anyone can plan very far ahead as there are so many things that cannot be predicted. It's easy when pregnant to think that choosing childcare is all about meeting the parent's requirements, however, after the baby is born and in the subsequent early years the child will display particular needs and these will change over time, making it unrealistic to expect yourself to work it all out in pregnancy. Although it's true that many types of childcare have waiting lists, people make decisions and change their mind right up until they go back to work (or decide not to!). For very many women this is an area where there is no choice: if you are the sole earner, for example, then you will feel you have to get back to earning as soon as possible. Whatever your situation try to allow for some flexibility after the baby is born as you may put yourself under undue pressure trying to meet everyone's needs: baby, family and work.

Remembering the time before baby

This may be a time where you have accepted yourselves as mother-to-be and father-to-be but there can still be time to recapture bits of pre-pregnancy life. It might be that you want to take on a particular project at work to reassure yourself that you can still hold your own. It might also be a time where if finances allow and you are feeling well, you can take a holiday. It can be very important to spend some time with your partner, not just being taken over by thoughts of the baby, but also just enjoying being together. Sometimes couples get caught up in 'I *must* do that before the baby is born' and set themselves overwhelming lists of things to do. It can feel as if life begins and ends on the expected delivery date! A new life for you all does start but a new sort of normality will establish itself too.

'I haven't had a chance to think about my pregnancy': building a relationship with the baby

As the pregnancy progresses, the baby begins to 'communicate' with you: little kicks and movements can be felt. Eventually when looking at your bump you may be able to make out how the baby is lying, where he likes to be. At ante-natal appointments you will hear your baby's heartbeat and at the mid-pregnancy scan you will see your baby in some detail: right down to the four chambers of his heart. You may also decide to find out whether you are having a boy or a girl. It becomes easier therefore to begin to imagine what this little person might be like. If he kicks a great deal, you might imagine him to be a lively, active baby and if this happens in the middle of the night, you may fear that he won't be a good sleeper! You may now be 'trying out' names and imagining many things about what your baby might look like or what his personality might be. For some women, especially in a second or third pregnancy, you may feel you haven't had a chance to think about the baby but it's never too late to start.

Many fathers-to-be find that there are few links with the baby during the pregnancy so beginning to get to know the baby can be enormously difficult as it still doesn't feel very real. This can be helped by trying to go to the scans and maybe an ante-natal appointment. However, partners can do one thing that mothers can't, which is to put their ear to the bump and listen to the movements of the baby! Mother and father can feel the bump together and experience the movements of the baby. All these things can help to bring the pregnancy to life for both parents and help them to begin to feel that they have a baby.

A generation ago this interest in the 'foetus' would have seemed bizarre to many people as the baby was really only seen as 'alive' once he had left the womb. Today we are much more aware of the womb as an environment and that we can influence the development of the baby by looking after ourselves. Some have taken this further and feel that they can begin to affect the baby's temperament and possibly even their intelligence by, for example, playing music to the baby while still in the womb. The evidence for this is equivocal and really so much less important than the fact that trying to get to know your baby and being aware of him before he is born can improve your relationship with him after he is born. Many health visitors who work with women who are not coping or are depressed in pregnancy find that where mothers are encouraged to think about or imagine their baby, this helps to prevent emotional problems post-natally. So if you want to talk to your unborn baby while doing the housework, then do it: it's good for you both!

Discovering the sex of your baby

It may seem very early to be thinking about the baby and how to care for him but often in late pregnancy women become preoccupied with thoughts of labour and birth so now is a good time to think about having a new person around the house.

It is possible now at the 20-week scan to find out the gender of your baby. This is not 100 per cent accurate as it is done by scanning the genital area and assessing what can be seen! Should you have amniocentesis, which involves chromosomal analysis, then identification is accurate. So how do parents-to-be decide?

For some, the decision is straightforward: if the information is available, we want to know. Others want the discovery to be part of the arrival of the new person. It seems to become more complicated where only one of the parents wants to know, or where there is a strongly held wish for the child to be of a particular gender. You may feel that in the latter situation, finding out will give you time to come to terms with any feelings of disappointment rather than facing this at the birth. However, without the baby there, it may be more difficult to assess the significance of this information, especially for a first baby. If you wait until the baby is born, then the gender is just one part of this new person that you have to get to know. Having a boy or having a girl may not be quite what you expected. It would be interesting to see more research into the impact that this knowledge has on parents. There is some evidence that it can have a negative impact on pregnancy and labour where the baby is discovered not to be of the hoped-for gender. Whatever you decide to do, it is worth being decided by the time you arrive for the scan and letting the sonographer know: many parents inadvertently find out because terms such as 'he' or 'she' are used or because they can see the genitals clearly.

'I'm not feeling that great'

Not all pregnancies are the same. Different women will have different experiences and the same woman can have very dissimilar experiences in different pregnancies. There may have been no sickness early on and life has been ticking over as usual right through. If you are very ambivalent about being pregnant, then it may be possible to continue to ignore the pregnancy well into the second trimester. Alternatively you may continue to feel a bit 'under the weather' throughout the pregnancy. You may be dealing with significant life events that have nothing to do with pregnancy. All these experiences are common. However, this shouldn't stop you from beginning to think about the baby and how your life will change.

It may be that you feel unhappy or depressed throughout the pregnancy or feel unable to contemplate the prospect of being a mother. You may feel it's best to just try not to think about things at the moment. If this is the case or if you have been having significant emotional problems before the pregnancy started then this can be a time to start doing something about it. As previously emphasised, pregnancy does last a long time and it may be a time to identify problems and look for solutions before the baby comes along. If you feel uncertain about what to do then it may be time to seek professional help. Try to speak now to your GP or midwife who can put you in touch with someone who can help. (See Chapter 4, 'Specific psychological problems in pregnancy' and 'Who can help?' on p. 83.)

The pregnancy coming to an end

Doctors and scientists have yet to discover the exact mechanisms that cause a pregnancy to end and labour to begin. Many women find that as the pregnancy draws to a close their mood may begin to change, perhaps becoming more unpredictable. This is probably partly due to the physical and practical changes that are going on. Your ever-increasing size may make your everyday life more difficult and more tiring. Sleep often becomes more disturbed now as you find it more difficult to get comfortable, as the baby lies on your bladder you need to get up to go to the toilet and probably too you find some of the anxieties of early pregnancy return. It is not unusual to become increasingly nervous about being a mother (or father) and more aware, especially when you stop working, of how your life is to change. Often, however, the fears and anxieties are focused around coping with the labour and birth. Health visitors and midwives who run parenting classes often comment that it can be difficult for a woman to think about anything other than labour in the classes. Although they are keen to cover the first few weeks of looking after a baby, parents especially mums-to-be, understandably, want to know about pain relief!

'I still don't think I'm ready to be a parent': changing roles for all

Psychologists often think about life in terms of events or stages and as a social world made up of roles and functions. The arrival of a baby brings together some of the biggest changes in these social systems that we are ever likely to experience in a short period of time. As we have said, the event of being pregnant often precipitates other life events such as choosing to move house, sometimes partners change job, or there is increased financial pressure. Both mother-to-be and father-to-be will also become 'parent', 'mother', and 'father': a new generation will be coming after them. You are no longer just a 'child' but a 'parent' too. For women having to lose the role of career person, even if only temporarily, may be significant in how they feel about themselves. These changes in status affect others too: your parents become grandparents; sisters and brothers become uncles and aunts.

What does it mean to be a 'mother'? Changes for women

The last chapter considered how we construct a view of being a mother and this will change in the course of the pregnancy. Where a pregnancy is progressing well with the mother-to-be reasonably happy with her situation, she is likely to gradually become more identified with other mothers, especially her own where the relationship was good. This may make it easier to begin to withdraw investment from other activities and begin to picture the new life ahead.

How certain or not you may feel about what it means to be a mother, clearly, certain changes of role do and perhaps have to take place. As a woman close to giving birth, you may be struck by the inevitability of change in your life. However, it may feel that for your partner change still involves choice: he may decide to stop football practice for those first few weeks after the baby is born but he doesn't *have to*, he can *choose* to. There may be a deep sense of loss for you about what you are giving up to become a mother and these feelings may become even more intense in those early months with your baby. Sometimes working until your due date may just be a way of avoiding these feelings and not thinking about the new life ahead. Gradually most women will begin to lessen their investment in the former life situation and begin to look ahead to the new situation.

What does it mean to be a father? Changes for partners

It may be late in the pregnancy that partners become more aware of the imminent arrival. Often it can be something as simple as planning to take some time off from work or cancelling regular activities that can bring it home that life is to change. This probably is a time when partners' roles begin to diversify, with the majority of fathers-to-be assuming the role of financial provider. For women with a good maternity package, who take no unpaid leave, the actual financial changes may be short-lived. However, this is often the first time that a couple have made such financial arrangements and the feeling for the woman can be that of 'dependant' even where the reality is different. This role of provider, especially where the mother will not return to work, can feel like a substantial burden, especially where the partner's earning opportunities are limited. Not all men expect to become the main earner and may feel their choices severely restricted by this new role. It may be that where there is ambivalence about becoming a father, the financial realities serve as a focus for those feelings.

It is not always true that becoming the main earner is a burden; in fact where the couple have had comparable careers, it may release them from a state of competition and rivalry. It may be that in assuming a role more like his father's, the man feels more secure, even if financially they are going to be worse off. For some men assuming the role of provider, with a partner at home with the children, brings a sense of 'family' that is familiar and makes it easier to assume the role of 'father'. However, with changing employment patterns in recent years many families are very dependent on the woman's wage and this can cause the partner to feel even more devalued if he cannot find reliable work while his partner is caring for a newborn.

'I thought you'd be delighted': changes for those around you too

Your pregnancy changes everyone's relationship to you and with you. This may seem like an enormous burden to shoulder but the acknowledgement of this state of affairs may help to explain why those around you behave in ways that surprise you and can be both positive and negative. Everyone needs time to get used to his or her new role. For a long-time friend who does not have children, it may signal a new and frightening change: will you still be close if you have less common experiences to share?; will you be able to empathise with and understand each other like you used to?

It also means a change for other family members: brothers and sisters become uncles and aunts, parents become grandparents. What may be upsetting for you as parent-to-be is where another family member is troubled by this shift. The dynamics and structure of all families are different: for example, in terms of who looks after and supports whom. It may be that you are playing a supportive or even caring role for a sister or a parent and the imminent birth may threaten that connection. There is a strong stereotype of the role of the grandmother. In an ideal world mother and daughter become closer through this shared experience of parenting and grandmother is there to provide emotional and much needed practical support. However, in our modern society where extended families are more the exception rather than the rule, this may be practically impossible. Where the relationship between mother and daughter has been poor, this can be the source of much disappointment as the mother-to-be perhaps hopes for but does not get this support.

Meg and Richard's story

Meg and her husband Richard came to see me when she was advanced in her pregnancy. Initially they sought help with arguments between themselves but it became clear that their fighting, sometimes physical, was generated by the pressure that their extended families were putting them under and they were being pulled in different directions to provide support. Meg's mother had been looking after her sister, a recovering heroin addict, and would constantly phone Meg if Alice were 'missing' for too long. Richard's father had died suddenly not long after Meg had become pregnant. Richard's mum expected him to call around every night after work and Meg was worried that this would not change after the baby was born. The more that Meg and Richard attempted to pull away and think about their new roles and responsibilities, the more their respective families seemed to fall into crisis.

Many people may be surprised by the reactions of their extended family to the pregnancy. Grandparents-to-be may be delighted about their new situation and yet find themselves reliving some of their own disappointments and problems of that time. This can translate into heavy-handed advice or not being available in a way that might have been hoped for.

Pregnancy is a time when you may be offered lots of 'advice' especially from your own and other parents, which may not always be helpful and may feel undermining. But it is important to remember everyone is going to be learning his or her new role.

Relationships: issues and problems

The pregnancy, especially towards the end, is probably where a divergence of role begins for the couple. All of a sudden the mother-to-be is at home ready to carry out a different role, which may awaken certain expectations for both partners. Does being at home equate with assuming all the domestic tasks? Often there is this expectation, although it may not always be articulated. If your mother always had the dinner on the table when dad got home, then this may be what you expect of yourself and may be what your partner imagines will happen. Consequently, late pregnancy may be a good time to sit down and discuss how you will manage the new domestic situation. It may be important to include in this discussion aspects of your life that you value and would like to retain after the baby is born. (See 'Discussion points' on p. 67.)

Pregnancy may bring to a head pre-existing relationship difficulties particularly where one person was ambivalent about the relationship prior to the pregnancy or where one partner has problems making a long-term commitment.

Alan's story

Alan had been with his partner for five years when she became pregnant. They had never talked about having children and although they rented a house together, Alan at times went back to live in a flat that he owned. He said that he had simply not thought about the pregnancy and spent more time in his own flat. He did not tell any of his family, friends or work colleagues about the baby and perhaps hoped it would all just go away. After the birth of the child he had still mentioned it to no one and began wondering how he might explain the situation to his family. His ambivalence about his baby was clearly related to problems in his own early life but these he had hoped to avoid thinking about too. His partner subsequently returned to her former husband, which offered Alan a route out. In some ways this made it more difficult for him to acknowledge that he was a father.

Often there can be a hope in pregnancy that the arrival of a child will bring the couple closer together. In fact, research has shown that all relationships deteriorate in quality with the arrival of children: good relationships remain good, however, just not quite as good. This may well be a temporary state of affairs while this process of change is gone through but it is important to have the right expectations: that child-rearing puts a strain on even the strongest relationships.

'When should I start maternity leave?'

Apart from the odd 'Superwoman' most women will take a period of maternity leave starting any time from 12 weeks prior to the estimated delivery date and carrying on for, in some cases, up to a year after the baby is born. Certain public services organisations like the National Health Service allow for up to one year of maternity leave. However, most of this is unpaid leave but service remains continuous. Until fairly recently women *had* to stop working at 28 weeks which was extremely frustrating for those who were willing and able to continue, and who wanted to 'save' the time for after the birth of the baby. Now maternity leave can start at any time after 28 weeks up until the day that the baby is born. This allows for individual women to decide what best suits their needs and their family's needs. However, unfortunately this has in some cases led to a misperception that all women can or should work until they're practically in the delivery room. The time to begin maternity leave is different for everyone depending on their work situation, their financial constraints, other children or responsibilities, and so forth. Nevertheless, allowing yourself some time to prepare practically and emotionally for the arrival of the baby should not be under-estimated. This amount of time will vary from woman to woman depending on her needs.

Inevitably as you prepare to leave work there is recognition that it will never be the same again. Even if you intend to return to work full-time as soon as possible, the situation will not be the same. Work *is* different when you have a baby to get home to. Although women are now 'free' to return to work, it is usually mothers who drop off and collect children from childcare. There can be a great sense of loss while preparing to finish at work. What will it be like not having to get up and go to work? Although we may at times resent the routine of work, routines are in fact very important for our psychological well-being. Work generally is very protective against depression: working women are less likely to be depressed than the unemployed or homemakers. Work provides a social world and for some their social life. Even where there are conflicts at work, this may still give a person a sense of involvement in life. It can be very frightening to see this disappearing, even if only for a few months. Possibly also you may feel resentful of other work colleagues, especially if you feel they might overtake you while you are away. Often colleagues have mixed feelings when someone is leaving: feeling perhaps envious that they are stuck here while your life is moving on and changing. Consequently your last weeks at work may be emotionally difficult.

Pregnancy's end

The end of pregnancy is the beginning of a new life but before the new can begin there are many endings to overcome. It is the end of a child-free life and a major shift of role to being a parent, a mother, and a father. There may be many aspects of your life; many freedoms that you feel you are about to lose. Strangely enough too, you may start to mourn the ending of the pregnancy. For those who have not enjoyed these weeks that may seem unbelievable, but where pregnancy has been a positive and 'safe' time, its ending may be mourned. This may be acutely so for a woman who acknowledges that this is her last pregnancy. For a partner such feelings can be perplexing especially where their thoughts are clearly elsewhere such as the quickest route to the hospital!

Who can help?

For general issues

Where you have a good relationship with your GP, then he or she is usually a good place to start. GPs should be able to advise you about the choices available to you in terms of ante-natal care and also be able to recommend more specific services for complications – physical or emotional.

Where you are interested in 'complementary' therapies, try to look for organisations that can recommend registered individuals rather than just picking a name out of the telephone book. Again, many progressive GPs will have lists of complementary practitioners such as acupuncturists or homeopaths. (The list of addresses on p. 181 contains contact numbers for the professional organisations.)

Throughout your pregnancy you will be seen by a midwife although your first 'booking' visit may not be until the second trimester. You will be given the option to choose 'hospital care' or 'shared care' where your routine ante-natal appointments are at your GP's surgery rather than at the hospital. Late in pregnancy your appointments will be weekly and you may appreciate being able to attend your local surgery rather than face possibly a long wait at a more distant hospital. Your midwife should be able to explain any aspects of pregnancy that you are concerned about, including emotional issues. However, in practice, most early visits to the midwife are fairly routine and swift, so it is best to write down a list of questions to take with you.

Your health visitor may also make contact with you towards the end of pregnancy and perhaps visit just to get to know you a little bit. It's much easier for them to assess how you are coping after the birth if they know how you were doing before.

For parenting classes

Everyone is entitled to attend parenting classes before the birth of their baby and these are usually run by the local midwives and health visitors. If you are lucky, they may take place at your surgery. Most classes are open to partners too. For partners who have mixed feelings about attending, there is research to show that the more partners are involved in supporting the mother after the birth, the less likely that mother is to get depressed. Parenting classes may help you to feel more involved in the pregnancy.

For those particularly interested, the National Childbirth Trust (NCT) run parenting classes in most areas. These classes tend to take a more informal and less medical approach. The NCT also runs a number of groups and events to support new mothers. If you don't have time for their ante-natal classes they can still put you in touch with other new mothers, so it is worth thinking about becoming a member of your local organisation.

Discussion points

1. Make a list of the aspects of your life that you value highly now. Cover the areas of work, social life, hobbies and family? What could you give up and what must stay?
2. How are tasks, especially domestic, currently shared out in your home and how were these decisions made? Are you happy with the current situation? How will these roles change, if at all, following the arrival of the baby?
3. What are your plans with regard to work? When do you want to start maternity leave?

4. Are you planning to return to work? If so, how much maternity leave will you be entitled to? How much of this decision do you feel will be made after the arrival of the baby?
5. If you stay at home or work part-time, what will your role be? Both partners should discuss their expectations.
6. What things do you feel you are gaining in becoming a parent and what things do you think will be lost?

4

Specific psychological difficulties in pregnancy

The popular image of pregnancy is of the parents-to-be perpetually in 'spring', a time of optimism, new replacing the old, new beginnings, and so on. It's not really like this: most women feel a range of different things through their pregnancy as do fathers-to-be. Chapter 3 has tried to identify themes and issues that are common to many pregnancies, but certainly not all. Reading so far, you may have found certain things that you recognised and others that were not your personal experience. However, for some couples, the entire pregnancy can be very different. A pregnancy can be seen as complicated for very many reasons: the mother may have a history of miscarriage or perinatal death, a previous termination of pregnancy or health problems such as pre-eclampsia. The baby may already be identified as having health problems or disabilities or may have been conceived through assisted conception. However, this chapter will concentrate on significant emotional problems. These may either pre-date the pregnancy or are generated by the experience of being pregnant.

Most people have heard of 'post-natal depression' and are prepared for the weeks after the birth possibly being difficult, but it still remains something of a 'secret' that depression occurs in pregnancy too. As was stated earlier, we enter pregnancy from a particular place in our lives, which might mean struggling to control alcohol or drug problems, or with a tendency to experience panic attacks or anxiety symptoms in certain situations. Pregnancy can re-ignite old difficulties such as problems with body image and fears about controlling your eating. For women who have experienced childhood sexual abuse, pregnancy may trigger or exacerbate a range of problems. For both parents-to be, where there were significant difficulties in their childhood, psychological symptoms may begin to surface during pregnancy. We have already talked about the changing nature of relationships in pregnancy and, understandably, in some cases, this leads to relationship problems or breakdown.

But don't we all feel fed-up at some point?

Research has shown that 15 to 20 per cent of pregnant women could be classified as having some form of psychological problem (Report of the General Psychiatry Section Working Party on Postnatal Mental Illness, 1992). But is it useful to separate out certain emotional reactions and call them 'problems'? It certainly would be difficult to draw a line and say that the thoughts and feelings of one group of pregnant women are different to the rest. At times all women are terrified by the thought of labour, or feel miserable or unattractive. It is more a question of degree: if you continually feel negative about the pregnancy, intruded upon by the baby, unattractive or that you will make a useless parent, then it is important to recognise that there is a problem and to try to understand the roots of it. Also it can be very undermining if you are told, 'well, everyone feels like this when pregnant' or 'you'll feel better when the baby is born', if it is clear to you that you are really struggling. Pregnancy can bring problems clearly into focus and it may help to give a sense of urgency to sort out things you have tried to ignore in the past.

Depression in pregnancy

Depression has been referred to as the 'common cold of psychiatry', that is it is something that most of us will experience at some point in our lives. However, if depression happens for the first time when pregnant, then this can be particularly puzzling for the mother-to-be and her partner, especially in a planned pregnancy. There is more recognition now that fathers-to-be may get depressed in pregnancy or after the birth of the child and that the emotional situation of one partner may affect the other.

What does it feel like?

We probably all know what it is like to feel really miserable but depression is something much more severe and pervasive. The main aspect of depression is a persistent low mood. Usually an extremely bleak outlook accompanies this: depressed people have a negative view of themselves, the rest of the world and the future. Many people find that their low mood is accompanied by what doctors refer to as 'biological symptoms': their appetite is affected, their sleep is disrupted with waking early being a common complaint, and they may lose interest in sex. Often the depression is much worse in the early part of the day and the person may feel unable to cope at all until the afternoon or evening.

How common is it?

Research has shown that as many as 10 to 16 per cent of women are depressed during pregnancy (Kumar and Robson, 1984; Johanson et al., 2000; Evans et al., 2001). There is often debate about whether depression is more common during pregnancy or post-natally, and whether depression at either time is any different than depression that women experience at other points in their lives. Clearly, there are many factors common to depression throughout the life cycle. However, this shouldn't deter researchers from trying to understand which particular aspects of pregnancy and childbirth trigger emotional problems, nor should it deter individuals from understanding which unique aspects of their experience of pregnancy and childbirth have led them to experience emotional difficulties.

Why does it happen?

The reasons that women become depressed in pregnancy are many. Some women may have a history of emotional problems and pregnancy may simply be another 'life event' that reduces that woman's ability to cope. Research shows there are also 'risk factors' specific to pregnancy. Problems may arise where the pregnancy was unplanned and the mother-to-be or father-to-be remain unhappy about becoming a parent. There may be guilt for the woman about a whole range of issues: previous termination of pregnancy or miscarriage, smoking and drinking in pregnancy or just not being good enough to be the 'perfect mother'. Poor self-esteem generally puts people at risk for depression but it may be the prospect of becoming a parent that triggers worries about 'doing it right' or feeling inadequate. Often if you are trying to live up to a perfect image of motherhood, then it is very easy to feel you have 'failed'. For example, if you are trying to give up drinking, then having one drink might confirm the belief that you are 'useless' and, conversely, lead to a drinking binge to cope with the feelings generated.

The physical changes of pregnancy can affect your mood: persistent sickness and lethargy can make it hard to engage in the activities that you find pleasurable or that make your life meaningful. A poor relationship with your own mother when you were a child can underlie depression. at any stage in a person's life but clearly becoming a parent yourself is often what triggers anger and sadness about your own lack of mothering.

Pregnancy is a different experience for everyone but most parents-to-be will feel some sense of loss even in a desperately wanted pregnancy. The mother will have to change her work situation, her body will change and probably will never return exactly to the pre-pregnancy state. Both parents will have to give up certain aspects of their life and take on new responsibilities. These factors can contribute to depression. Also for some parents-to-be there may have been a hope that a baby would 'make everything alright' in the relationship and already in pregnancy it may be clear that this is a false hope.

What can I do about it?

Whatever the reasons for depression, the experience can be terrible. Depression can turn your whole world 'bad', making everything seem hopeless. You may feel completely at odds with the world if everyone around you is telling you how wonderful it is that you are pregnant and you feel desperately unhappy and unsure why you feel like this.

- *Understanding the problem:* It really is important to try to begin to unravel these feelings and identify what problems underlie them. It may be that there are some things you can do nothing about: a relationship that has broken down or financial problems. Usually there are things that you can change: perhaps in terms of how you view yourself or how you relate to other people. In order to find your way out of depression, it may be necessary to seek professional help to start to identify which things you can change. Trying to look at how your (negative) thinking or underlying false beliefs can affect how you feel is known as 'cognitive' or 'cognitive-behavioural' therapy. Your GP should be able to tell you what types of mental health services are available locally in the NHS.

Samantha's story

Samantha's relationship had broken down irretrievably and she was to be a single parent which she had always insisted would not happen to her child, as she felt she herself had missed out through the death of her father when she was a toddler. She felt she was clearly a useless person otherwise she wouldn't have ended up pregnant with a man who didn't love her. Samantha needed help to look at what she could achieve as a parent. Although she could not bring her child's father back, she could still provide a warm and loving home for her child with lots of positive aspects. In time too she might help her child to understand something about her father and why he had left. She also became more able to acknowledge that her partner had chosen to leave and had not wanted to take responsibility for his child: that didn't make her a useless person.

- *Social support:* Another important factor in depression is the lack of a supportive relationship with a confidante and therefore it may be important in pregnancy to rally as much social support as you can so that you have people to call on at times of need.
- *Life events:* For many women, pregnancy is one life event too many. This can be particularly acute in an unplanned pregnancy where couples sometimes rush into making a number of other decisions too such as moving house or getting married.

Julie's story

Julie came to see me towards the end of her second pregnancy. She told me she was coming to see me now as she was well aware of the risks of post-natal depression and she was worried she might experience it because of all of the stress that she was currently under. She was working very long hours as a GP and the practice was struggling to cope with a rebuilding project that had run into problems. The builders had left a trail of problems behind them and her colleagues expected her to take an equal share in all of the after-hours meetings and paper-work. Julie felt exhausted, she had far too little time for her first child and she felt totally unsupported by her colleagues. Julie was able in time to acknowledge that she was distressed and struggling now. She

> *had hoped I would agree with her 'post-natal depression' diagnosis because she really didn't feel she had time to be depressed now but hoped to 'sort herself out' during her maternity leave.*

Anxiety and panic attacks during pregnancy

In Chapter 3 much was said about fears and anxieties particularly early on in pregnancy. It is very common to be fearful about labour, about your capacity to be a parent or the health of your baby. However, if you are continually gripped by these fears or experiencing regular panic symptoms, then you may need to look a little deeper into what is going on. Chapter 8 looks at understanding and dealing with anxiety symptoms. Below is a brief outline of issues to do with anxiety but Chapter 8 is essential reading for a fuller understanding of the issues.

What are panic attacks?

At some point in their life most people will have a panic attack. You may start to shake or tremble, feel your heart racing, feel short of breath or start to hyperventilate. You are likely to interpret these as signs of some imminent danger, 'I'm having a heart attack' or 'I'm going mad' and these panic thoughts will cause you to leave the situation – run from the supermarket or leave the meeting at work. This extremely unpleasant experience will usually lead you to avoid the feared event or situation, 'I'll never go in a lift again'. Unfortunately the next time you approach a similar situation the panic will start again.

Panic attacks are often an aspect of most anxiety problems. Sometimes people talk about dealing with stress and often if someone is feeling 'stressed', they are experiencing symptoms of panic and anxiety. Whatever you call these symptoms, the process of beginning to understand them is the same.

Why do panic attacks happen?

There is some evidence that for those who have a history of anxiety problems, their symptoms can improve in pregnancy. If you are experiencing regular panic symptoms, then this can actually have negative effects on your pregnancy. High levels of anxiety in pregnancy have been linked to higher levels of hypertension in mothers. Often when people are experiencing panic attacks it is because problems are not being addressed or fearful thoughts or situations are being avoided. If you are terrified of hospitals, then it doesn't help to avoid the problem until you go into labour. Facing up to the problem might be as simple as needing to discuss your thoughts and feelings with a trusted friend or partner. It may be that you need to seek professional help if there are more complicated issues that need unravelling or if you need specific help to deal with the anxiety symptoms. (See 'Who can help?' on p. 83.)

What is OCD?

Another type of anxiety problem is obsessive-compulsive disorder (OCD). This involves the performing of certain compulsions or rituals, such as repeatedly washing your hands or checking that the door is locked. These rituals are performed in order to avoid or neutralise anxiety-provoking thoughts. These thoughts are so fleeting that you may not even be aware of them. Many people are so anxious they only focus on the fact that if they do not check something, they are overwhelmed by panic and these awful feelings are abated by the checking. However, the rituals can become so time consuming that they bring normal life to a standstill. One lady who worked as a secretary constantly checked her typing to see if she had inadvertently typed a rude word. Eventually she had to give up working as she could finish so little work in the course of a day. The thoughts that underlie these rituals are usually fears about saying or doing something terrible. In pregnancy it seems that often the avoided feared thoughts are about harming the baby or being exposed in some way as a bad person. Very often people do not come for help with OCD until the problem reaches unmanageable proportions. (There are probably many people leading very happy lives who have mild OCD and just about manage to keep the checking going.) However, pregnancy and the imminent life changes may make the performing of rituals impossible. For example, some people with OCD get ready in the mornings in a specific order and if any small factor goes wrong, they will have to start again from the beginning. Not very easy to do if you have a newborn baby. These symptoms tend to get worse when experiencing other life events and there is evidence that OCD gets worse during pregnancy.

Obsessive-compulsive disorder does respond well to therapy but it is important to get the right sort of help. Research has shown that therapy needs to specifically address the behavioural management of the symptoms, counselling alone will not help you to deal with the rituals. Your GP will be able to refer you to a clinical psychologist or other therapist competent in cognitive-behavioural therapy.

Kim's story

Kim came to see me in the latter stages of her second pregnancy. She was almost housebound because of her obsessive-compulsive problems, which meant that everything that came into the house had to be thoroughly washed. Kim was so fraught with worry that she couldn't really acknowledge that there was anything excessive about her behaviour, she was more concerned about the amount of time she was spending cleaning. She had her first child at 16 and with the help of her mother had managed to care for her daughter and keep on her job part-time. She still lived with her mother but her partner was keen for her to move in with him eventually when they could afford to do so. Kim had been managing quite well before her maternity leave had started but now every time her daughter stepped outside the house she had to change her clothes and bathe her. All shoes had to be washed with bleach before they could come into the house.

These problems had probably been around for some time but Kim had just about managed to keep up all the rituals before. It may have been the imminent arrival of another baby or the fear of moving on and leaving her mother's house that had brought things to a head. However, the most immediate concern was helping Kim to get some sense of control over these cleaning rituals and to try to manage and understand her anxiety problems.

Eating disorders and body image

During adolescence women's bodies go through enormous changes as our sexual characteristics develop and our body reaches its full adult size. These changes to our body can affect how we see ourselves, how happy we are with what we see and they can contribute to the development of an eating disorder. For most women, watching their body change in shape is not easy. The majority of women are probably 'watching what they eat' and so eating in pregnancy can be problematic for most. Every woman will resolve this challenge in different ways. The early pregnancy can be most difficult, as once women 'look pregnant' they become more accepting of their changing shape.

Anorexia nervosa

The psychology of anorexia and bulimia is complex and looking at how and why it develops is beyond the scope of this book. However, it is helpful to look at how women with eating problems may approach pregnancy. As discussed earlier, few young women today allow themselves to eat freely and many young women and men are preoccupied with dieting and body shape. Most women are striving to be a bit thinner, to have a smaller bottom or would like bigger breasts or fuller lips. However, despite their dissatisfaction, most just get on with their lives and these issues just tend to surface at certain times. In anorexia nervosa the issues run much deeper; many women have a totally debilitating obsession with controlling their eating which is the driving force in their life. Often this means they are never able to form adult attachments or have children. For some their starvation has led to infertility.

The seriousness of anorexia is sometimes under-estimated and if you do become pregnant while actively experiencing symptoms of anorexia nervosa, then it is extremely important to have as much support in place as possible. A pregnancy when you have anorexia should be considered a 'high risk' pregnancy medically and be closely monitored by the obstetrician. Most women with severe eating problems are torn in pregnancy between the desire to feed and protect their unborn child and their terror of weight gain. It is important too therefore to be in touch with someone who can help you challenge the psychological aspects of this problem. If you have previously seen a therapist, you should contact them for further help or if you have never sought help before, then the pregnancy might motivate you to try to change things. See your GP first, who will know which services are available locally.

Many women have problems with their eating or maintain a low weight but do not want to be labelled as having 'anorexia' or an eating disorder. The reasons, however, for acknowledging the problems and seeking help are important. Where women are of significantly low weight when they conceive, then their babies are at greater risk of poor growth in utero, low birth weight and premature birth and a much higher rate of neo-natal death. There are at least two ways of deciding if someone is underweight. In current diagnostic criteria for anorexia nervosa it is said to be 'body weight less than 85 per cent of that expected for height and age. Most doctors will calculate someone's Body Mass Index or BMI. You can do this yourself by multiplying your height in metres by itself. You then take your weight in kilograms and divide it by the answer to the first sum. A score of below 20 would be considered underweight and a score of above

30 overweight. Around 25 is a healthy weight. Over 40 would be considered very overweight. These factors can clearly lead to further physical/developmental problems for your baby and there is evidence to show that these babies often go on to have poor growth throughout the first year.

In anorexia nervosa there are issues about feeling that you can control the shape of your body by controlling eating, consequently, pregnancy will greatly raise your anxiety. To allow a baby to grow inside of you or to eat freely may be very frightening. This is why it is important to get help and support as soon as possible.

Alicia's story

Alicia who was in hospital for treatment of her anorexia told me that she longed to be pregnant again as it was the only time she had ever eaten freely. She was able to imagine that everything she ate went directly into the baby and therefore she would not have gained any weight by the end of the pregnancy. Despite this she ate very little during the pregnancy and was very 'frail' after the birth of her baby and found caring for him an enormous struggle. Her husband had to take an extended leave from work to care for both of them.

Bulimia and binge eating

Binge eating is so common in the 14–25 age group that it could be considered normal behaviour for young women in the twenty-first century. It is also very common for bingeing to be followed on occasions by vomiting or the use of laxatives or diuretics. Binge eating is always associated with restricting your eating: people binge because they restrict and avoid food, leading to cravings and preoccupations with 'forbidden foods'. It is a very acceptable social norm for women to perceive themselves as unable to control their eating. Many will say 'I can't have chocolate in the house or I will binge on it.' However, many fail to link this to the fact that they don't eat regular meals, therefore feel hungry and increase their risk of bingeing. A binge is followed by guilt and further abstinence, which then perpetuates the cycle.

Ideally, during pregnancy, eating should involve regular meals and no long periods of abstinence and certainly no vomiting or laxatives. Most women do seem to be able to get control of their eating during pregnancy or allow themselves to lose the control and eat freely for the sake of the health of their baby.

Bulimia is a more serious form of binge eating where the starving/bingeing cycle is regular, as are vomiting and the use of laxatives. At the more serious end of the scale bulimia is associated with a general impulsiveness, incidents of self-harm and drug use. Bulimia can also appear in low weight/anorexic women. Generally, women with bulimia do not have the problems with conception that is seen in anorexia but many women with bulimia may have conceived impulsively and be ambivalent about the baby. Many manage to control the bingeing and vomiting while pregnant but relapse after the birth of the baby. There is less research into bulimia in pregnancy but there are reports of miscarriage rates being twice as high in bulimia sufferers. Babies of these women do better than the babies of women with anorexia but mothers have more problems coping with the care of the baby rather than problems with the pregnancy.

Consequently it is very important to assess the nature of your eating problems very early on, perhaps when planning a pregnancy. If you have anorexia or bulimia, then it is important to get professional assistance both from the obstetrician and some form of psychological support to try to reduce the eating problems while pregnant.

Katrina's story

Bulimia and other eating problems are often seen as 'teenage problems' but very many women continue to struggle with eating problems throughout their adult life. Katrina came to see me for help with bulimia. She had never sought help before but she was expecting her third child and finding it difficult to control the problems in the way that she had in the previous pregnancies. Katrina had two teenage sons who both excelled in sport. Her husband was out every night with the boys, taking them to various clubs, training and events. Katrina said that although she was enormously proud of them and of the efforts of her husband, she felt 'left out' and increasingly uninvolved in their lives. She had a very demanding job which she said had helped her to control her bingeing in the day but in the evenings, alone at home, she was regularly bingeing and vomiting. The pregnancy had been something of a surprise but both Katrina and her husband had felt it would be 'good' for her to have another baby. However, the reality was that Katrina felt even more trapped at home and worried about how she would cope with a baby when she was nearly 40.

Katrina struggled greatly to control her eating and rarely made it to the appointments we had made. After the baby was born, however, her mood improved and she felt that she was coping much better. She was enjoying the baby and feeling more involved in the family again.

Substance use, aggression and acting out

In Chapter 3 there was discussion of how to manage drinking and smoking in pregnancy. Clearly, some women and/or their partners will need the support and guidance of a specialist drug advisory service if they are regular users of non-prescribed drugs or heavy drinkers. These behaviours can have very serious consequences for the development of your baby and your pregnancy will definitely need to be monitored closely.

If women are twice as likely as men to be depressed, it is clear that men are much more likely than women to express their own distress in terms of alcohol and drug use and violence. Many women may find themselves pregnant with a partner who uses drugs and/or is violent. For Meg and Richard, who were mentioned earlier, the pregnancy led them to seek help for Richard's angry outbursts and he was very motivated to change. However, sometimes a pregnancy may lead to much more 'acting out' in the partner: staying out late, excessive drinking, late night rows, and so on. Often where the man's own experience of parenting has been very poor or he has seen his own father behave in this way, then this can be how anxieties about becoming a father manifest. Sometimes with some help and support the father may be able to feel that he has some resources to parent a child. However, if both parents are struggling, then this may result in the relationship ending or remaining poor.

Kate and Grant's story

Grant came to see me for help with his drinking and alluded to the fact that it helped him to manage his temper. He eventually admitted that he was separated from his partner who was six months pregnant. Grant said that he and Kate had always had arguments and they had often erupted into physical violence. He wanted to control his drinking because he felt he might soon lose his job as a bank manager because 'he couldn't hack it any more'. He said that heavy drinking was almost part of the job and everyone did it. Grant was stuck in a situation where until he was willing to stop drinking he wasn't able to begin to identify the problems that led him to hide behind alcohol use. He wanted to return to his partner but he couldn't stay sober long enough to sort anything out.

Survivors of childhood sexual abuse

With increasing awareness of the occurrence of the sexual abuse of children, more women and some men too are willing to come forward and seek help in dealing with the consequences of abuse in childhood. Often women come for help with depression or an eating disorder and later on in the therapy reveal that they were abused. Many women I have worked with have been able to have a sexual relationship with someone where they were very 'detached' or cut off from their feelings but it was when they become involved in a serious relationship that the sexual relationship triggered anxiety, flashbacks or depression. For some women the thoughts of being pregnant and going through labour are terrifying: women may fear feeling out of control or are terrified of being examined or touched. These fears can trigger intense anxiety or flashbacks. Many survivors of childhood abuse also worry about their ability to be a parent: will they be too over-protective of a child? Or they worry about not being able to protect them. Some women have dealt with the abuse by asserting a very rigid control over themselves and could not contemplate the idea of a baby growing inside of them. If you look at the statistics for childhood sexual abuse, then there are clearly many women who never seek professional help. Contemplating a pregnancy or struggling with a pregnancy might be the time to think about seeking help.

Maya's story

Maya came to this country to marry her husband who was the son of a family friend. Very soon after their marriage she became pregnant and was pleased to give birth to a healthy baby boy. However, during her labour she experienced many complications and had to have an emergency Caesarean section after failed attempts at a ventouse delivery. She took quite some time to recover but after a few weeks all was well. When her baby was a couple of months old, her husband was keen to begin a sexual relationship again. However, she said that whenever he tried to climb on top of her she felt as if she was being smothered and had flashbacks to how she had felt as they had prepared her for a general anaesthetic to deliver the baby. At the time her blood pressure had risen and she feared for her life as she went under the anaesthetic. This in turn had reawakened memories of being a very young child and how her teenage brother had come to her room in the night and put his hand over her mouth to keep her silent while he abused her.

Maya made very substantial progress in therapy. The terrible secret that she had hidden for years had finally been brought out. Maya had a lot of things to discuss in terms of how she had feared for her life in labour and how this had mirrored the fear she had felt as a child. Eventually, Maya was able to resume a relationship with her husband but at this time she did not choose to tell him or anyone else about the abuse. She greatly feared what her husband might do if he found out.

Dealing with the effects of childhood sexual abuse

There are many different ways that people come to terms with past experiences of sexual abuse. It is always important to let people do this in their own time and their own way. Some women find solace in reading the stories of other survivors of CSA. Many books have been written by or for survivors of sexual abuse and three are listed in the reading list on p. 188. For others, individual or group therapy can be helpful. This might involve exploring the effects that the abuse has had on your life, looking at destructive ways of coping that might have resulted, i.e. drug use, and trying to move on from feelings of guilt and shame. Not everyone needs the same sort of therapy. Suzanne was referred for help with the effects of CSA and was three months pregnant when she came to see me. After telling me of her experiences as a child she decided that I could 'look after this story for her' until she had more time to deal with it in the future.

Looking beyond pregnancy

For many women and their partners, becoming a parent is a challenging time. Pregnancy does, however, last quite a long time, which does give people the opportunity to adjust and make changes before the baby arrives. The pregnancy can give a sense of urgency or new motivation to deal with old problems. Pregnancy also does have an end, so if you are not enjoying it, then you may eagerly await your labour. You may feel you have come a long way in these 40 weeks and yet you are facing another new beginning. Your labour may last only a few hours but for most it is probably the most significant transition you will ever make.

Who can help?

The experience of significant emotional problems in pregnancy can be overwhelming and it really is important that you make the first step and try to talk to someone about how you are feeling. Perhaps that might be your partner, a friend or relative. As we have said, psychological difficulties are very common so maybe people won't be as surprised as you think. They may just be relieved that you are opening up about what is wrong. Sometimes you may need more help than a friend can provide so it may be time to approach your GP who can put you in touch with people who are trained to help. If you don't 'gel' with your GP, you could try speaking to the midwife or health visitor many of whom will have had specific training in dealing with emotional problems and also are very used to dealing with women who are having difficulties.

Most GPs are aware of local mental health services and many now have a counsellor or psychologist attached to their surgery. Although waiting lists are usually long, most people will try to see a pregnant woman as soon as possible for an initial discussion at least.

Birth

During pregnancy most women will spend a great deal of time antici-
pating, thinking about and planning for the birth of their baby. The
experience of labour is very different for all women and it is difficult to
predict who might have an arduous 24-hour labour and who may have a
quick drug-free birth.

There are a number of choices to be considered in pregnancy about the
birth of your baby: where should I have my baby? Who do I want present?
Do I want a water birth? An epidural? Many of these initial choices will
depend on what facilities are available locally as well as the preferences of
the parents. Many of the decisions made in pregnancy may be overturned
when labour arrives (or doesn't). Late in pregnancy a baby may appear to be
breech and an elective Caesarean may be recommended when you had
planned a home birth. The expected contractions may not occur and labour
may be induced. You may have contemplated an elective Caesarean because
of fears about giving birth and have a quick labour with little intervention.

The unpredictability of labour doesn't mean that you cannot prepare for
it. Learning about what is likely to happen in labour, the stages it
progresses through and how you might manage the pains will all contribute to your experience of labour. Thinking about your partner's
involvement and discussing his role can help improve the experience for
both of you. Research has shown that a number of factors can reduce the
length of labour and therefore the need for intervention. This includes the
quality of the support that you receive in labour so preparation is not a
waste of time. For some women the struggles of labour may be over-
shadowed by the immediate crisis of a baby needing special care. For
some (around 1 per cent) labour may end in the loss of a baby.

This chapter will focus on some of the key issues for labour: types of care, managing pain and managing your feelings. It will also touch on the issues of complications and loss.

So what exactly is a domino? The choices and decisions surrounding birth

During pregnancy your ideas will have begun to form about where and how you would like to give birth. Some women will have strong ideas and expectations from the start whereas others will feel confused and uncertain about what the choices are. It is not the purpose of this book to cover these in detail and certainly services are very different from one area to another. Your GP will initially outline what the local services are and your midwife will be able to explain these in more depth when you have your initial 'booking' appointment. These 'choices' are driven to some extent by what is available locally.

Where do I want to have my baby?

Most women will probably not be offered a choice about where they want to have their baby. On the first visit to the GP to announce the pregnancy, the doctor will want to get you 'booked' at the local hospital. From their point of view this is to make sure that you receive all the appropriate care and do not 'fall through the net'. You will be booked for a hospital delivery, at the local maternity hospital unless you specifically ask for something different. Most parents-to-be at this stage will not have thought very far ahead and will not be aware of what choices might be available. It is possible to visit local services, maternity wards usually do 'tours' for prospective parents and some parents-to-be do change their mind about the hospital as the pregnancy progresses. Sometimes the decisions are overturned as the circumstances of the pregnancy change, for example, a breech presentation late in pregnancy may mean you are booked for an elective Caesarean section.

Hospital birth

The vast majority of women today give birth in hospital. This trend grew in the twentieth century to the point where almost all babies were delivered in hospital but is beginning to change with growing numbers of women wanting to have something different from the rather anonymous experience of going to a hospital and being delivered by someone you have never met before. It isn't just a question of hospital versus home delivery; women want more choice within the hospital setting. Change is still in its infancy but what choices are available?

There may be more than one maternity unit available. If you are within a reasonable distance of more than one maternity ward, you might like to look around both and decide which feels best or which offers the things that are important to you. The hospital midwives may be able to offer different types of delivery, for example, there may be facilities for a water birth on the labour ward. The service may be able to offer a 'domino' birth: domiciliary-in-and-out delivery. This involves the midwife joining you at home and assessing the progress of the labour and then going in to hospital with you for the delivery. Then if all is well, you can return home six or so hours after delivery. In practice, this type of service may not be available to all women due to resourcing problems. This combines some of the aspects of home and hospital deliveries that women want. In an ideal world all women would have had some contact with the midwife who delivers them since research shows that this can decrease the length of labour and the need for intervention. Generally there is a drive within the NHS to reorganise services so that more women are delivered by a midwife whom they have actually met during pregnancy.

Deciding to go to hospital is not a cut-and-dry issue. Towards the end of pregnancy it is something to discuss with your midwife and at any ante-natal classes you attend. You can also phone the hospital ward once labour has begun and assess your situation with them. Despite what one might see on TV, women rarely have their babies within minutes of feeling a contraction and with a first baby it is not unusual to be sent home from hospital after a couple of hours because you are not in active labour or because labour often slows down if you arrive at hospital in the early stages. This may be because it is difficult to keep active when given a room with a bed in it and not much else.

If you choose to have your baby in hospital, you can also opt for 'shared care' and have your ante-natal appointments at your GP's surgery.

Independent midwives

Many midwives who want to offer a different sort of experience to that available within the NHS operate as independent midwives either individually or in group practices. They may offer to deliver you at home, in a separate midwifery unit or at your local hospital. Wherever you decide to have the baby, this offers you the support and continuity of seeing one or two midwives throughout. Unfortunately the NHS rarely provides such services and the cost of this type of care means it is only available to a tiny minority.

Home births

Deciding to have your baby at home may not be met with a great deal of enthusiasm by your family or the professionals. Only a very small proportion of women have their babies at home and it is not recommended as a standard option for all mothers, especially first-timers. It has been assumed in recent years that hospital is the safest place to have a baby but is this correct? Increasingly, evidence is growing to show that home birth, in an uncomplicated pregnancy, is at the very least no more risky than hospital delivery which carries with it different sorts of risk.

Many doctors do not encourage first-time mothers to give birth at home. You may have problems convincing those around you too that it is a good idea. Seeking help and advice from the local midwives might be a good starting point. As one of these will be delivering you, it is important to feel reassured that they are supportive. Other organisations such as the National Childbirth Trust (NCT) may be able to offer advice and information.

The politics of birth

Birth is an aspect of women's lives that has been the subject of debate for a number of years now. There are arguments over where is the best place to have a baby, whether medical professionals use too much intervention and why the rate of Caesarean section has increased rapidly in the past 30 years.

In the latter half of the twentieth century it was argued that birth had become over-medicalised and under the control of (usually male) doctors. This led to the growth of women's movements such as the National Childbirth Trust (formerly the Natural Childbirth Trust) which campaigns to increase women's choices and offers support and information to pregnant women with the aim of avoiding unnecessary intervention. In this country the control of childbirth has been fought over for centuries. The growth of the medical profession in the seventeenth and eighteenth centuries led to control moving into the hands of men and out of those of local women. Developments such as the invention of forceps in the nineteenth century and the use of morphine needed the medical practitioner to administer them. Gradually, therefore, the hospital became the safe place to give birth with the doctor present to oversee. If you go into hospital, medical intervention is available, should complications occur. However, if you are in hospital, intervention is *readily accessible* and therefore more likely. More intervention, for example, an epidural, can slow down the progress of labour and lead to the need for further intervention such as forceps. So deciding where and how to have your baby today is not a simple question and might mean quite a bit of information gathering and thought before you can be clear about what is right for you.

Caesarean section

Around one-fifth of all births now are by Caesarean section. There has been a rapid rise in the past 30 years or so in the use of Caesarean section and the rate has risen even faster in the past five or so years. It is too early to say whether the trend has peaked or is set to rise even further. Some might argue that Caesarean section (C. section) is performed for medical/clinical reasons and therefore it is not an issue of general concern, however, the rate has risen so sharply over such a short period of time that it has caused debate over why, and whether all these operations are clinically necessary.

There seem to be no definitive explanations for this trend but a number of factors are perhaps involved. Caesarean birth has become safer since the advent of local/ epidural anaesthesia and this may have led to it being seen as a less risky option medically. There may be a trend to intervene early rather than risk later complications that would then require emergency C. section under general anaesthetic. Women also perhaps perceive Caesarean as safer than their mothers would have done and therefore are more willing to opt for it. For example, few breech babies are now born spontaneously: most women are offered and accept a Caesarean delivery. They will be conscious while their baby is delivered and able to have some contact with him immediately after birth.

So if it is perceived to be less risky, has a situation developed where women are 'demanding it', as has been suggested in the media? A current stereotype is of the 'too-posh-to-push' mother. She is the assertive middle-class mother 'demanding' a Caesarean partly because a planned Caesarean delivery fits better into her busy life schedule. There is some research to suggest that obstetricians are prepared to offer C. section to women who request it for reasons other than necessary medical ones. If this is the case, then we have to ask, what are women's perceptions of birth currently such that they are beginning to choose surgery over labour with all the possible complications and restrictions (i.e. you can't drive for six weeks after a Caesarean)? Has the common perception of birth become that it is really too painful and risky and that Caesarean is the safe pain-free alternative? The increased C. section rate is a world-wide phenomenon, therefore, some of these cultural explanations could only be part of the picture. There have been reports by doctors suggesting that women need re-educating about the need for Caesarean section but until all the factors in this puzzle are understood, it is not clear who needs re-educating. Studies, particularly in the USA, show that increasing Caesarean rates are related to fears about malpractice prosecutions: doctors are intervening earlier rather than risk complications and possible litigation. Individual doctors and different institutions have differing rates of C. section and one American study showed that the rate of C. section correlated with the malpractice claims status of the doctor. Clearly there are issues about how clinicians assess risk.

If we want more women to go through labour, then also the right type of services need to be available. Hospitals currently cannot provide the level of staffing that would allow more women to choose home birth, domino delivery or have continuity of care so that they are delivered by a midwife involved in their ante-natal care. Research shows that the poorer the quality of care, the longer the labour and the greater need for intervention. If women have less personal and less than adequate care, it seems far more likely that intervention will occur. In these less than perfect clinical situations, the fear of litigation probably makes early intervention more likely too.

There are certain factors that clearly will have led to the increase: having had Caesarean at first birth, then it becomes clinically more likely for a subsequent labour due to concerns about the effect of labour on the scar. Many women may therefore opt for a planned Caesarean rather than have the dual difficulties of labour and then a Caesarean. We are delaying the age of first pregnancy, and increasing maternal age makes Caesarean much more likely. As yet it is not clear whether an increased C. section rate is necessarily a bad thing: we don't know yet whether maternal and child outcomes are better than with a lower C. rate. After all, what exactly are appropriate clinical reasons? If a woman is terrified of labour, possibly following a previous traumatic delivery, then perhaps a Caesarean is the most appropriate course, since intense fear can cause complications in labour.

Clearly, this debate is complex and we are waiting for better research and advice. So it is within this climate that women have to try to understand and make choices about their birth.

Labour

Late in pregnancy it is not unusual for women to become preoccupied with anxieties about labour: will I know when it has started? When should I go to hospital? There can be an increased sense of panic about getting things done before the baby comes or an increasing lethargy, a sense of feeling fed up with the pregnancy and wanting the baby to arrive. Partners may now also be concerned about the role that they will have to play. Some may be worried about what is expected of them or how they will react to seeing their partner in pain or distress. Others may be focused on getting their partner to the hospital quickly.

This sense of uncertainty about labour is understandable. 'Full term' is now considered to be anywhere from 37 to 42 weeks. This is a long time to live with the sense of 'any minute now'. Passing your due date can also increase a sense of frustration and many women become anxious for something to happen. There may be many early signs of labour – a show of blood or stronger Braxton hicks' contractions (Braxton hicks are the painless contractions that some women feel throughout pregnancy) – and then these recede. Has it begun? Are you any closer to the birth? Obviously, yes, but is this labour?

How will I know when it has started?

Despite all we know about pregnancy, it is still not clear what the precise mechanisms that trigger labour are. The beginnings of labour can be very different for different women and you may well think it has begun a number of times before it actually progresses. The technical definition of being 'in labour' is that the cervix has dilated by 2 to 3 centimetres. Some women at this stage may have experienced few indications that they are in labour and may not in fact recognise themselves to be in labour until further down the line. Other women might go into hospital in great agony feeling ready to deliver, only to be told that they are 'not actually in labour yet' as they are not 2–3cms dilated.

Signs of labour beginning

The signs of labour commencing are:

- a show: loss of blood and/or mucous;
- backache/period type pains;
- regular and strengthening contractions;

- waters breaking;
- nausea/vomiting/diarrhoea.

Labour may begin very suddenly with your waters breaking but more likely, especially for a first birth, the signs of labour will begin gradually perhaps over a period of days. Clearly, eventually you will know you are in labour because the symptoms will increase and progress: contractions will become more regular and more painful. Your midwife will help you towards the end of the pregnancy to think about what will happen as labour begins, when to go to hospital and who to contact if you are at home. Here obviously attendance at parenting classes can be invaluable in helping you to understand what is happening to you and how to deal with the experience.

What about going overdue?

Your due date may seem like a very important marker during the course of the pregnancy, however, as previously mentioned, there is in fact a five-week window in which your baby's arrival would be deemed normal. Many women are very concerned about going 'overdue' and possibly having their labour induced. There may be some women who now feel so desperate to have the baby that they are relieved when offered a date for induction.

Once your due date has come and gone, there is no precise time at which intervention might occur: it very much depends on the individual pregnancy and how it is deemed to be progressing, however, pregnancies don't usually go beyond two weeks overdue. A medical induction involves using drugs (hormones) to bring on labour. This can be combined with rupturing the membranes i.e. actually making your 'waters break'. These procedures are often employed once labour has started spontaneously but fails to progress or progresses slowly. Many women are emotionally distressed by the idea of such interventions for a number of reasons. It is perceived by many to be unnatural and more painful than spontaneous labour. It can also make women feel as if they have 'failed' in some way, that therefore they are not having the 'natural' birth that they wanted. They may also feel that the birth has from the beginning been wrested from their control. This can lead to a sense of powerlessness and therefore the expectation and acceptance of more intervention.

It is crucial in labour to retain, as much as possible, a sense of being in control and involved in what is happening to you. Just because labour is started artificially doesn't necessarily mean that you cannot progress with the rest of the labour as planned (obviously not if you wanted a home birth). The birth partner can be very important here in terms of trying to assess the mother's mood and trying to help, reassure and encourage her.

What about raspberry tea?

As discussed, the mechanisms that cause labour to begin are somewhat elusive. Although hormones will definitely bring it on, clearly, other factors also affect the beginning of labour. It seems to be common practice that women who are medically fit with their baby fine and well are given a date to come back to the hospital for induction rather than being taken in immediately. Often being told you are to be induced is closely followed by the beginnings of labour. Perhaps the baby was about to appear anyway but it is interesting to speculate on what psychological mechanisms may be at play. But what can you do if you are sitting at home waiting for that baby to arrive and feeling concerned about the possibility of being induced? Many other factors are thought to help the onset of labour and other women may share with you how their labour started. Some of these are dietary: the drinking of raspberry tea (available from health food shops) or eating spicy foods is suggested to help labour begin. There is no scientific evidence for these and obviously it's not a good idea to do anything that you don't enjoy or anything to excess. Sexual stimulation is said to bring on labour in some cases. One could see how this might be possible since sexual activity encourages the release of certain hormones and may also cause some contractions. Increasingly as women are looking to alternative methods of induction there has been some research evidence for the efficacy of acupuncture in inducing labour.

With all of these things, however 'natural' they might seem to be, obviously it is important how each individual approaches the situation. If you have previous experience of acupuncture, and know the acupuncturist, this might be helpful for you. However, drinking lots of raspberry tea, if it makes you feel sick, or approaching an acupuncturist for the first time when you are two weeks overdue may not be the best way of approaching labour. It is important to try to approach labour in as calm and relaxed manner as possible. This will facilitate feeling more in control, more able to make choices, more able to actively participate in your labour.

Has it really started? Stages of labour

So you have woken up in the night with the arrival of a contraction, others follow intermittently but they continue to come. Your labour has begun. In order for your baby to be born your cervix, which is the neck of the womb, needs to soften and open to allow the baby's head to pass through into the birth canal. This first stage of labour lasts until you are 'fully dilated': this is where the cervix has expanded to about 10 cms. Stage 1 can last a couple of hours or 10–15 hours in a first labour. However, your first stage may appear even longer since you are only said to be 'in labour' when your cervix has reached 2–3 cms dilated. So in fact you may feel as though you are in labour for some time only to be told that it hasn't yet started.

The first stage of labour often ends with an urge to push but there may be a period of transition where the contractions seem to stop, the mother may feel nauseous or actually vomit. Although this might be unpleasant, it does signal the beginning of the much shorter second stage where the mother has to push out the baby with the help of her contractions. Some women feel an overwhelming urge to push. Others need support and encouragement from the midwife to push during a contraction. This stage ends with the delivery of the baby. The third stage of labour is the delivery of the placenta.

What can I do about the pain?

Many writers do not use the word 'pain' when talking about labour partly because they feel it doesn't describe the experience of labour fully and that it gives mothers negative expectations. These expectations lead to fear and therefore the experience is more likely to be poor. Clearly the 'pain' of labour is a much broader experience than just the physical sensation, it is emotional too, and it includes many thoughts and fears as well as the contractions. However, you are unlikely to find a woman on a post-natal ward who will say that their labour wasn't painful. Therefore it does seem useful to talk about pain so that one can get information and be prepared for how one might deal with that experience.

What is pain?

Pain at its simplest is a series of messages sent from a site of injury to the brain to alert the individual that some form of action is necessary. It is an adaptive response to our environment: if we are being bitten by a predator we need to fight them off or stem the bleeding. If we have put our hand in a flame, we need to remove it quickly. But people experience pain in different ways and to different degrees. Any pain is made up of both physical and psychological aspects and therefore everyone's experience of pain is different: we talk of people having different pain thresholds. This does not mean that you are 'making it up' as some mistakenly believe, but it means that the actual physical reaction of pain is mediated by psychological factors. If you put your hand into a bucket of ice eventually you will remove it because of the pain. If you are watching your favourite film at the same time you will probably not remove your hand so quickly: being distracted has changed your experience of pain. Clearly it is also important to have learnt something about potential dangers and this learning changes our behaviour: we have stored memories of pain. For example we automatically use oven gloves: we remember that the saucepan handle is hot, it will hurt me, therefore, I must use a glove. We have also learnt about how to respond to an injury. As a child, if your mother becomes distressed and terrified every time you fall over, then this will affect how you experience pain. It is likely that you will feel that any injury is something to be feared and that you will experience pain more negatively. (This is not always true: some may learn to disregard the response of their parent, as it does not concur with how they feel.) However, your experience of pain will be mediated by what you have learnt and experienced as a child.

Psychologists call this the *biopsychosocial model* of pain, that is, it has some biological aspects, some psychological aspects and some social or learned aspects.

For many women their labour will be one of the most intense 'pain' experiences they ever have and yet despite this, the majority of women go on to have a further delivery.

In the section on morning sickness we talked about the interplay of physical and emotional factors and clearly a mixture of physical and emotional factors will affect the whole experience of labour. For example, as you approach labour you will probably be anxious which will cause physical effects such as your muscles tightening, your breathing becoming shallower which will release adrenalin and further speed up your physical arousal. Psychological research has shown that the more physically relaxed you are and the more able you are to think non-panic thoughts, the lower you will rate your experience of pain. Consequently, your experience of labour will be more positive and probably less painful if you can be aware of your fears and not let them take over completely. It may be that for most of us this is not easy, especially in your first labour.

What types of pain relief are available?

So if we accept that labour may be painful and that we may approach it with some trepidation, how can we best manage this experience? How can we approach it in a less fearful and more prepared way (and hopefully therefore experience it as less painful)? There are various ways of managing pain in labour, beginning with the least invasive such as breathing exercises or getting into the bath through to major drugs, and at the extreme end of the spectrum a Caesarean section.

Pain relief is something you will want to discuss with your midwife, in ante-natal classes and gather as much information as possible. Just as everyone's experience of pain is very individual, so is each person's approach to pain relief: it is as well to keep this in mind when people are giving you advice. Also, it is clearly difficult to decide beforehand what you need since you don't know how you will feel, how long your labour might last or how it might progress.

Ways of relieving pain and surviving labour

- relaxation, massage, breathing, movement and position, getting into water;
- feeling and thinking in a more positive way, feeling in control to some degree, feeling supported by a birth partner or familiar professionals;
- acupuncture, homeopathy, water-birth;
- transcutaneous electrical nerve stimulation or TENS;
- entonox or gas-and-air;
- pain-relieving drugs, e.g. pethedine;
- epidural anaesthesia.

The least invasive, early in your labour

You might well find yourself uncertain at first whether labour has begun. You are perhaps just having period-type pains and feel a little 'unusual'. Midwives will usually advise you simply to carry on as normal at first or to try and sleep if it is still night-time. Despite this being very good advice, most women are probably emotionally 'charged' at such a time: wondering what will happen next, feeling a mixture of fear and excitement. This is the time, before it becomes too painful, to perhaps try to do some relaxation exercises to try to focus your thoughts. It is important where possible to try and stem panic thoughts, possibly by trying to replace them with more calming images. At the same time once labour is established, it is useful to keep upright and gently active in order to 'help' the labour along. This is a time where your partner may be able to massage you, or you may wish not to be touched, so make it clear. You may choose to get into the bath and relax or begin to make your preparations for the day (if you have a partner to call home, or other children to make arrangements for).

Once labour is established, you may still have a number of hours to go. Try to continue to stay relaxed mentally alongside not becoming too inactive physically. Remaining upright or not lying on the bed helps. This can be difficult in the hospital setting if the bed takes up most of the room.

Actively managing the pain: acupuncture or homeopathy

You may also be planning to use acupuncture, or homeopathy for pain relief, in which case you should use the services of a registered practitioner. The addresses for the associations of homeopaths and acupuncturists are given on p. 181. These organisations will have lists of appropriately qualified practitioners and they will be able to give you advice about what to ask. You should always ask someone about their experience and training when you are looking for a practitioner outside of the NHS. There has been in recent years some good research evidence for the effectiveness of acupuncture in managing pain, in shortening first stage labour and therefore in reducing the need for epidural. This research is still in its infancy but the signs are positive. Obviously, acupuncture is probably best suited to someone who already has experience of it and has a practitioner that is known to them.

Transcutaneous electrical nerve stimulation or TENS

TENS is another method of drug-free pain relief. It involves strapping small pads to the back and then using a little control pad to pass a small amount of vibration/electrical stimulation. TENS has been used for various areas of pain management and many women find it particularly helpful in early labour. In terms of research results, the jury is probably still out. More recent (and perhaps more rigorous) research has found it to be no more effective than a placebo in terms of reducing use of other types of pain relief and in shortening the first stage of labour. You may have heard of placebo pills that contain no active ingredient. When researching other types of treatment a 'dummy' intervention is given to a similar group of people. It is made to resemble the active treatment in every way. This then tells us whether there is anything effective about the treatment or whether it is just better than nothing at all.

However, many women like TENS because it helps them to feel in control. You can press the button and 'zap' the pain when the contraction comes. It is always useful to have a number of strategies to try. TENS might work for you. You may get a chance to try one of these at an ante-natal class and you certainly need to work out how to put it on before you go into labour.

Entonox or gas-and-air

Feeling that you need more powerful or a different type of pain relief is sometimes the factor that helps you to decide that it is time to make the move to hospital (if you are having the baby there). Entonox, known to most of us as gas-and-air, is obviously only available at home if you are having a home delivery. It is used during contractions to ease the pain. It has no adverse effects on mother or baby but it can make the mother feel a little nauseous or woozy.

Pain-relieving drugs and epidural anaesthesia

Once in hospital it is possible to have pain-relieving drugs such as pethedine. These drugs can have side effects and can affect the baby. Many women especially at first labour will have an epidural anaesthetic. This usually provides complete pain relief but can have the effect of numbing your abdomen and legs and you may need a catheter to empty your bladder and a drip to maintain fluids. It is important to get lots of information in pregnancy from your doctor and midwife about these procedures and their side-effects in order to make a decision about what is right for you. You should do this during pregnancy, as it will be difficult to take in the information when you are in labour. Many women now do choose to have an epidural and in a long labour the pain-relieving effects can prove a significant boost to your morale. The effect of epidural can be variable and you may be quite immobile. The pain-relieving effects need to be balanced against the fact that epidural can increase the length of labour as it can mask the urge to push in second stage. This can in turn lead to further intervention such as forceps or possibly a Caesarean.

Feeling involved in your labour

Being given a menu of different types of pain relief may seem quite overwhelming. How do you know what is right for you? Over the course of the pregnancy through consultation with your midwife and through attending ante-natal classes you will begin to form some sort of idea about what you might do, however, probably most decisions are made in labour depending on the particular experience of labour that you have. You will also get lots of advice from other women: with the birth experience being so intense people can often be very convinced that what was right for them is right for you. People will tell you that: 'You must have an epidural!' or 'You should avoid all drugs because they make you feel so out of control.' It is useful to listen to other women's stories but it is hard sometimes to assess them objectively. Some women may be clear from the outset; I don't want any drug intervention or a water birth is how I would like the baby born. When you actually go into labour you might feel quite different. That TENS machine that you practised with so avidly may seem far too fussy and to be getting in the way. Your partner may have planned to massage your back and now you can't bear him to touch you. Be ready to change your mind. It isn't a sign of failure to accept intervention. This is where the role of the birth partner is so important. He or she can ask the midwife/doctor for some information about why they are suggesting a particular course of action and can check out with you if that is what you really want.

Having a successful labour is probably most about being able to deal with the situation that arises and not having your ideas too firmly fixed beforehand.

'That's not what I wanted'

Throughout this book childbirth has been discussed as a life event, a time of significant change for you and those around you. How we deal with change and the unexpected is significant in terms of how we survive emotionally. The ability to be flexible is therefore important. Trying to approach labour with an idea about what you do and don't want is important but more important is the ability to accept the unexpected and adapt your thinking. Is it really a failure if you have an injection to induce labour? Once it has happened, it is important to move on and concentrate on staying involved in the situation.

Very often, after delivery, women are upset and disappointed about what happened in their labour. Being prepared for disappointments and the unexpected may help to lessen that feeling. Try to remember that in six months' time whether or not you had an epidural will pale into insignificance. One way that we deal with uncertainty about things is to be adamant that we are right and that there is a right or wrong answer. Some people will be adamant that any use of drugs or intervention is wrong, others will insist that it is unsafe to give birth at home or without constantly being strapped to a monitor. It is important to get information but then to make your own decisions in the light of your own labour. If you have a two-hour first stage then you won't be having an epidural, if you have been in first stage for 24 hours it may be medically essential to speed up the labour for your sake and the baby's. You may never get into the enormous water bath that has been filled. If your blood pressure is raised or the baby's heart rate falls, a Caesarean may become necessary.

It may be that after the birth you need to go back to your GP or midwife or someone whom you trust and discuss what happened and why and how you feel about it. Most women and their partners spend a great deal of time in the weeks after the birth recounting their experience in great detail, especially to other new parents and this may be a helpful way of coming to terms with the experience, both good and bad. It may be that these spontaneous discussions are a significant aspect of how we assimilate the experience.

The role of the birth partner

Not that many years ago the place for the expectant father was pacing outside the delivery room. This trend was probably reinforced by the increasing medicalisation of birth over the twentieth century. However, there is a wealth of evidence to suggest that the presence of a supportive person (not necessarily the father/partner) during labour improves the outcome in many ways. A birth partner is associated with, for example, shorter labours, less intervention and a more positive experience of birth. It also seems to improve the partner's attachment to the child. That is not to say that some partners aren't overwhelmed or troubled by the experience. However, despite all these positives, many partners feel unsure of what is expected of them and feel fearful about what might happen. Many birth partners now attend ante-natal classes or appointments with the mother-to-be and this will at least help to highlight some of the things that might happen during labour.

As every pregnancy is different it would be impossible to set out the definitive birth-partner's guide, however, here is a list of some of the roles that the birth partner might be called upon to perform.

Partner's checklist

- *Practical tasks*: especially early in the labour, e.g. arranging childcare for older children, collecting together the things to take to hospital, attaching the TENS machine.

- *Listening* to the mother, asking her what she needs/wants and 'translating' for the midwife.
- *Acting for* the mother where necessary: not taking over but doing things she can't do or wants the birth partner to do.
- *Encouraging and interacting*: raising the mother's spirits, asking her questions, encouraging her.
- *Looking after* the mother.

When a woman goes into labour, she may be very relieved to be able to hand over all practical tasks to someone else so that she can concentrate on her labour. It is important to check out whether this is the case, as some mothers may find the focus of collecting their things together a useful distraction in the early stage of labour. That leads us on to the second issue of listening to the mother and at times translating for the professionals around. Remember, the birth partner knows the mother and the midwife doesn't, so if the birth partner feels the mother is not speaking up, for example, then the birth partner should ask her what she thinks or wants so that he can tell the midwife. In the early stages of labour the midwife will not stay with you throughout and you will have time alone to discuss any decisions that need to be made. At times the birth partner may actually need to act for the mother, doing things she can't or doesn't want to do; that might be as simple as helping her change her clothes or it might mean asking to speak to a doctor for advice. The birth partner may need to work hard to encourage the mother to 'keep going' during the labour or to raise her spirits if it is all too overwhelming. In a hospital situation it is very easy for the labouring woman to become very passive: if you are exhausted and have had drug intervention, it may seem easier to just 'let it all happen to you'. However, the partner can play an important role in encouraging the mother. For example, she may need a lot of encouragement to really concentrate on pushing if she is exhausted.

The midwife or doctor may seem much more knowledgeable and powerful and the birth partner can feel as if they are in the way or a spare part. But try to remember that the partner is a significant person in the birth and that the mother needs the partner to be involved. Try to stay active and involved particularly if the mother seems deflated or confused. Giving emotional support is of primary importance. If the partner can continue to encourage and reassure the mother, this will help lift her mood. This is not always easy since the partner may well be feeling overwhelmed too.

It is very important too that the partner looks after his own needs. It may seem unsympathetic to tuck into a sandwich when the mother is struggling with contractions, however, the labour, especially a first, may last a very long time and the partner needs to remain able to support and help the mother, and not be preoccupied by the fact that he is starving.

Of course, it is not possible to predict what will happen or how the partner will behave, but being prepared to have to take part will probably help the partner feel more involved and therefore hopefully more positive about the whole experience.

'I've done it all before' or 'Oh, no not again'

So far we have been emphasising first labours and the thoughts and emotions that go with it. However, this may not be your first pregnancy and therefore your feelings may seem very different. Second or third time around mothers usually feel that they have far less time to think about what is happening and have spent far less time concentrating on this pregnancy than they did first time around. You may have also encountered the attitude from others that 'you've been through it all before' and therefore you should 'know what to do'. It shouldn't be forgotten that every pregnancy is different and so too is every labour. Statistically it might be true that subsequent labours tend to be shorter but that doesn't necessarily mean it will be easier. You may feel much more tired and less focused on giving birth than you did before and you may feel preoccupied with existing responsibilities. Many women approach the situation with unpleasant memories from the previous labour and perhaps are feeling much more fearful than they did before. There may be a sense of inevitability about it: 'I had a Caesarean last time so I'm bound to have another.'

Alternatively, a previous experience may have encouraged you to do it differently this time. You may have attended birthing classes again, chosen a home birth this time, decided to have acupuncture if you need to be induced. A distressing experience first time may galvanise you into action to prepare yourself in a different way.

The biggest issue for subsequent pregnancies is usually managing your multiple responsibilities. If you are feeling unprepared or unsupported concerning labour, it is going to be a less positive experience. It is important to recognise that you still need the active support and guidance of a birth partner. Even though there can be other children to think about, it is important that you have the support as well. This may be even more true as you may feel you are more tired, less relaxed and your thoughts are more split than they were first time around.

Complications and loss

Complications and special care

Every labour is different and there is not just one type of experience that could be considered a normal labour. Partly too complications are to do with your perception of the events. If you have a planned Caesarean section, perhaps for a breech presentation, then you may not perceive your labour to have been complicated even though you have had full medical intervention. However, there are events in labour such as your baby being 'in distress', or your blood pressure rising too high, that lead to further intervention which can in turn leave you feeling distressed and troubled by your labour. In the next chapter we will be looking at recovery from the birth and considering how these events may affect your recovery.

Even where your labour was uncomplicated, some newborn babies will need 'special care' or in more serious circumstances 'intensive care'. This may involve just a few hours of closer observation or it may involve many weeks of specialist medical and nursing care. The reasons for this type of care are most often to do with babies being born premature and being of low birth weight. Some babies are 'small-for-dates', that is, less mature than their age would suggest. Some of the other reasons for needing special care, such as breathing or feeding problems, are usually related to the baby being early or small and therefore his organs are less mature.

Jenny's story

Jenny gave birth to her daughter Imogen at 32 weeks following an emergency Caesarean section. This was her first baby and she had had a reasonably uneventful pregnancy until her waters broke unexpectedly. She went into hospital where the doctors became concerned about her health and that of the baby and therefore the delivery was carried out. Jenny said that she had been completely unprepared for the birth of the baby. She had left everything until she had planned to start maternity leave at 36 weeks. Her mother, who lived abroad, had planned to come over and support her around the birth but she did not arrive until the baby was a week old. The baby was in Special Care for eight weeks and Jenny and her husband felt their introduction to parenthood was like 'caring for a sick relative'. It was hard to feel connected to this tiny baby that Jenny said seemed so unlike a baby. She found the hours in the hospital a relentless stress followed by a

> *deep emptiness every night when she returned home without Imogen. Three weeks after the birth Jenny's mother returned home and Richard had returned to work. It was then that Jenny began to feel depressed: her experience was so unlike her expectations. Instead of walks in the park pushing the pram, she spent endless hours watching her baby sleeping and feeling like 'a fish out of water' in the institutional environment of the hospital. Six months after Imogen came home Jenny began to have the experience of parenthood she had hoped for. As Imogen became more active, Jenny began to enjoy her daughter and this helped to lessen her sense of loss.*

Stillbirth and neo-natal loss

It is almost impossible to imagine the grief of parents who have lost their baby. Around 1 per cent of pregnancies end in the loss of the baby: either the baby dies later in pregnancy, during birth or in the first month of life. Often the reasons are never clearly known, especially where the baby dies late in the pregnancy. Sometimes there are concerns during the pregnancy about the viability of the baby once he has left the womb but, more often than not, the child dies before, during or shortly after the birth without warning. The most common causes of death are serious congenital abnormalities or very premature birth. Some women have the trauma of having to give birth to the baby knowing that he has already died. Sometimes the death occurs in labour, for example, because the cord is around the baby's neck when he enters the birth canal. However the baby is lost, the impact can be profound and long-lasting.

The reactions to this type of loss can be very varied and research has shown that parents demonstrate high levels of psychological distress particularly in the first six months after the loss. This may manifest as depression or anger or withdrawal from usual activities and relationships. Dealing with the loss is very individual but many parents find it helpful to keep a few mementoes such as a lock of hair, a nametag, photos or other personal items that carry special memories.

All new parents seem to need to recount their birth story over and over and this seems to be a helpful way of 'processing' or coming to terms with this very unique experience. For parents who have lost their baby, this is probably more important but often others find this difficult: they are embarrassed, don't know what to say or do, or feel that they 'should have moved on by now'. What grieving parents need is for those around them to talk to them, to hear their story and to offer whatever practical support might be necessary. Also they need to be given time to recover. It is this factor often that leads people to seek professional help, as they still need to go over what has happened. Parents usually feel that others don't understand and particularly don't understand how long it can take to grieve the loss of a child. A year or so after such a loss some parents do feel they are recovering but the research suggests that many are still struggling two to three years later. Recovery is also hampered by other problems, for example, if you have difficulties with your relationship, if generally you have a lack of support in your life or if you have had psychological problems in the past. Sometimes parents recognise that they need help because something is getting in the way of them moving on. Recovery can be hampered by feelings of guilt or blame that can be very difficult to discuss with a partner.

Sharon's story

Sharon came to see me about two years after the death of her baby Alfie. Her appearance was striking, as she was dressed totally in black. At a routine visit to the midwife at 39 weeks no heartbeat was found and a scan revealed that her baby had died. Her labour was induced and she said there was no explanation found for his death. Sharon appeared very depressed and found it difficult to talk freely about anything in our first meeting. Sharon had five children from a previous relationship and Alfie was the first child of her current marriage. She said her husband had wanted her to come and see me because he was worried about her. He felt that it was time now for them to put away the clothes that she had prepared for Alfie and to dismantle the crib that was in their bedroom. Sharon said she didn't really want to argue with him but she still felt the need to go and sit next to the crib and look at the clothes and think about Alfie.

Sharon did take a long time to come to terms with her loss. She felt unable to move on and come to terms with what had happened partly because she was troubled by terrible feelings of guilt. These feelings related to having missed some of her ante-natal appointments with the midwife. Also Sharon's family had disapproved of her choice of her husband and had warned her that marrying someone of a different culture wasn't 'right'. Sharon felt that for these reasons the outside

> *world would blame her for the loss of the baby. It was easier to imagine*
> *what it would have been like if Alfie had lived rather than face her own*
> *anger with herself and others.*

Moving on from loss

For most parents who have lost a baby, embarking upon another pregnancy will prove an anxious time. There is probably no 'right time' to
consider another pregnancy since this very much depends not just on
grieving and physical recovery but on all the other factors that go into
deciding when is the right time to have a baby. Often in a subsequent pregnancy there is an emotional detachment from the pregnancy: an
unwillingness to invest emotionally and risk experiencing the intense feelings of loss again. There is some suggestion too that the children born
following a loss can have more physical or emotional difficulties due to
over-anxious or over-protective parenting. It is probably important therefore to be prepared for the possibility of problems so that you are more
ready to face them should they arise.

Who can help?

During your labour and birth you will come into contact with a wide range
of professionals especially if you have a hospital birth. However, your
starting point is your GP and the local midwife who should be able to
advise you about local services. Visit your maternity hospital and do the
ward 'tour', where you can ask questions, see the labour ward facilities
and the post-natal ward set-up. Find out about local ante-natal or
parenting classes from your midwife as here you will be given in-depth
information about questions such as 'what is an epidural' or 'when should
I go into hospital?'.

If you are seeking help with questions following your labour or struggling to come to terms with the loss of a baby, then both your GP and
midwife should be able to answer questions about what happened and
why. Following the loss of a baby, the consultant obstetrician will usually
discuss the details of what happened or any information from the post-
mortem.

When recovering from loss, the support of family and friends can be
very important. At some point in time you may wish to speak to a

bereavement counsellor and your GP or midwife may be able to advise. Not everyone wants or needs this type of help after a loss. For some people it is months or years later that they decide their grieving is 'stuck' or going on for too long. It may be another pregnancy that makes someone feel that they have issues to resolve and that they need to talk to someone.

On p. 181 there is a list of addresses of organisations that support parents who have lost a baby. This type of support, from others parents who have been through similar experiences, can be very helpful.

Discussion points

This chapter raises numerous issues in terms of thinking about where and how you might like to have your baby and how you will manage the experience of labour. It might be useful to discuss some of the following points:

1. Where would you like to have your baby and what types of facilities would you like available? What is available locally? From where/whom can you get more information?
2. What preparations do you need to make? What ante-natal classes are available?
3. Who should/will be able to attend?
4. What do you know already about different types of pain relief and what appeals to you? What helps you to relax? Do you have any experience of dealing with pain and, if so, how did you cope?
5. Who is around to help? Who will be your birth partner? Who can help out in those first few days? What specific help will you want: someone to do some shopping? A relative to stay at the house? Or would you prefer not to have visitors?

6

The first few days

Your baby arrives at last!

It is impossible to describe those first few moments after your baby is born since the experience is so unique and personal. For the majority of women their first meeting with the baby will be as it arrives into their arms as soon as it has been delivered. It can be a moment of elation, of enormous relief and great joy. That is not to say that it is universally a pleasurable experience since many couples may be feeling so overwhelmed or exhausted that they hardly know what to think. Should your baby be unwell or born very early, there may be no relief at all as medical assessment gets underway and the baby is taken from your arms. These few moments are particularly precious since it is a time to meet this new person before other events take over: the initial assessment of the baby, the need for special care, the delivery of the placenta, the need for stitches and all the other immediate and more medical concerns.

Going through your labour may have been an intense and exhausting experience both physically and emotionally. Had you just run a marathon, you would now expect to put your feet up and have a well-deserved rest, however, labour is just the first lap of an incredibly long journey. Whatever way the baby arrived, however exhausted and physically ill you might be, the task of parenting begins immediately. You will experience from the start, at its most intense, the dilemma that is central to parenting: the balancing of your own needs versus that of the baby's. This factor seems central to what makes the first few days such an intense and at times difficult experience and why almost all mothers will struggle emotionally at times in the first few days.

In this chapter we will look at what might happen in those first few days. What are the immediate tasks of parenting: how often should I feed the baby? How long will he sleep for? Should I pick him up when he cries? Is this something that we learn or that comes instinctively? Second, the mother has to recover from the labour. You may have stitches, a catheter, bruising and discomfort and most likely you will feel exhausted. There can be a roller coaster of emotions too. Most women initially are on something of a high: they are immensely relieved the baby has arrived and appears well, the pains and emotions of labour have disappeared and they are sharing those first few moments with their baby. This, however, can very suddenly be replaced by tears, frustration and uncertainty as the reality of caring for the baby dawns and your tiredness and discomfort kick in. We will consider the emotional situation of those first few days looking at the range of reactions such as 'baby blues' through to the serious but rare problem of puerperal psychosis. What is the significance of these emotional reactions and will they have long-term effects? How does an attachment develop between parents and their baby?

A time of intense and rapid adjustment

Often books on pregnancy seem to trail off after the sections on childbirth and perhaps many parents-to-be are not interested in reading much further during pregnancy. However, it does seem important to emphasise that the emotional experience of those first few days may be very intense. The labour and the birth of the baby are an important *part* of the transition to parenthood but only a part. A time of high emotion and rapid adjustment continues in those first few days. It would be wrong, however, to give the impression that this is necessarily a negative experience. The difficulties are almost always outweighed by the joys. What is remarkable is to see a woman who, in labour, was feeling intensely distressed, half-an-hour after the baby is born sitting contentedly holding the baby as if she had been doing it for years. Two hours later the same woman may be in tears at her struggle to 'latch the baby on' to the breast. The first few days are about all of these conflicting feelings, emotions and experiences. You are now learning your new roles of mother and father. First, let's think about the baby.

Forming a relationship with your new baby

During labour it is possible to lose sight of fact that there is a baby arriving at the end. You may feel so caught up in dealing with the contractions or feel numbed by the effects of drugs that you may feel you just want to recover but the baby is thrust upon you, often literally. Suddenly you have a totally dependent and needy baby whom you must learn to care for.

Your first few moments with the baby

New mothers spend an enormous amount of time just looking at, holding and exploring their new baby. Parents quite spontaneously look in great detail at this new person trying to get to know him and beginning to respond to him. The baby's tiny movements, expressions and vocalisations promote a response in the baby's parents and the very rudiments of communication begin here. Parents quite spontaneously start to respond to the baby: he is not simply held in a completely static way. The psycho-analyst and paediatrician, Donald Winnicott emphasised the importance of not interfering with this process which happens naturally and spontaneously. It is not something that parents need to be taught. If you watch a new mother she will spontaneously change the baby's position in response to his movements. She will often move her head or face in a similar way to the baby, especially if the baby is awake and alert. If he begins to cry, she will attempt to soothe him, perhaps by rocking or beginning to feed. This clearly is a learning process, the parent does not know what to do yet, but the curiosity and eagerness to learn seem almost instinctive.

Mothers will often be encouraged to feed the baby if he is awake and both seem relaxed. The baby may of course be sleepy (especially where there has been use of medication during labour) and therefore you may just watch him sleeping. For many new parents this is a wonderful time of elation, of feeling closer to each other as a couple and feeling enormous relief at the baby's arrival. However, it isn't always so, depending on how you are feeling at this point: exhausted, overwhelmed, confused, and so on. The bond with your baby is not always instant and in many ways you are strangers who need to get to know each other. Not everyone feels that connectedness straightaway, it can take much longer but that doesn't mean it won't develop. Unfortunately the hospital setting may not always facilitate this process. Staff may not be available to help or may be preoccupied with different concerns.

The initial assessment of the baby

Very soon after holding your baby the medical staff will wish to check the baby is well and complete an Apgar score (see *The Pregnancy Book* for an explanation of the Apgar score), clip the umbilical cord, clean the baby and put on an identity tag. Most of this may happen while you are delivering the placenta, being prepared for stitches or whatever medical procedures are necessary for you.

What can newborn babies do?

In recent years as research techniques have improved we have become much more aware of the capabilities of newborn babies. We have known for a long time that babies are born with primitive reflexes. Clearly the sucking and rooting reflexes are crucial to a baby's survival. If you stroke a baby's cheek he will turn his head and start to suck. Babies can hear from birth but remarkably they quite quickly learn to recognise their mother's voice from others. They are able to focus on objects at a certain distance, this distance being roughly that between them and their mother's face during feeding. Quite quickly too they are able to discriminate their mother's face from others. It is perhaps important to remember when you are finding it a struggle, that your baby is primed to get what he needs i.e. to feed and also to develop a relationship with you. So he will be helping out too: babies appear almost programmed to develop relationships. Most of their early behaviour − crying, making eye contact, vocalising or smiling − is all designed to engage the parent and form an attachment.

Getting to know your new baby: bonding/attachment

Often when professionals use words like 'bonding' parents feel intimidated as if this were something complicated and technical but really we are talking about you and the baby getting to know each other and feeling a closeness or connectedness. Many parents will say that they did not feel an immediate bond with their child and for some it may take many months to have that strength of feeling. The development of an attachment between parent and baby is important as this relationship provides the secure base from which the baby can go on to develop and explore his world. He does this secure in the knowledge that usually if he feels hungry or upset, his cries will bring the intervention of his mother or caregiver to provide the necessary comfort and security.

There can be a number of reasons why the relationship with your baby doesn't get off to the best start. For the mother it may have been a traumatic delivery, she may have been ambivalent about becoming a parent, or it may be the result of a poor relationship with her own parents in her early years. It may be that usually you are a very anxious person and the sense of responsibility overwhelms you at this stage. There may be lots of reasons that you feel less 'in tune' with your baby and therefore find being with him less rewarding. If you are terribly anxious about how much milk your baby is getting and how much weight he is gaining, then you will be less relaxed and able to enjoy feeding him.

As well as issues that you bring to the relationship, there are also factors to do with the baby. If your baby is born healthy and a good size, begins to feed quite easily and sleeps a lot, you are much more likely to feel relaxed and able to respond to your baby and in turn feel that you are making a reasonable start at being a mother. However, if the baby seems to come out screaming or doesn't seem to want to feed, you are more likely to feel anxious, miss the signs that the baby is giving you and start to feel scared and uncertain about your ability to look after the baby. Feeling close to the baby is going to be hampered by feeling overwhelmed by the needs of the baby. Should your baby be in an incubator, you may find it much more difficult to obtain the closeness with the baby and to manage your fears about what is happening to him. You will be encouraged, however, to feed your baby and hold him as much as is possible.

An attachment to your child almost always develops and if you don't feel it straightaway, try to relax and give yourself and the baby some time to get to know each other. If you are concerned try to speak to your midwife or health visitor (see 'Who can help?' on p. 131).

Jenny's story

Jenny first came to see me when her daughter was about three months old. She spent most of our first session in floods of tears and almost everything that she tried to talk about would unleash her tears (during this time her daughter was sleeping quite happily in her car seat). Jenny and her partner had eagerly awaited the arrival of their daughter and were very pleased to have a healthy baby. However, Jenny was concerned that since the birth she had felt very 'cut off' from her baby. Although she said she knew she loved her, she didn't feel that things were 'right' between them. She felt particularly guilty about this as she said Hannah was such a good and contented baby. It became clear that Jenny was so anxious about every aspect of looking after her baby, that it had practically paralysed her and she barely found time to get dressed in the day let alone start going out and meeting anyone else or looking after herself. It became clear in time that Jenny had always been very anxious and the new responsibility of the baby had overwhelmed her coping resources. She was making life very hard for herself as her anxiety meant she missed any cues from her baby. Despite the fact that Hannah was gaining weight Jenny could not convince herself that Hannah was getting enough milk. She was supplementing her breast-feeding with extra bottles 'just in case' her milk wasn't enough and also because she had a better idea of how much milk she was having. She was having her weighed every week and would leave the baby clinic feeling devastated if Hannah had not gained 'enough' weight. These worries were stopping her from enjoying her interactions with Hannah or getting to know her baby and trust her reactions.

With some exploration and challenging of her self-critical thoughts Jenny began to gain confidence as a mother. Her partner and those around her were crucial in helping her not to escalate a small worry into a 'disaster' such as when Hannah later caught a cold and had a high temperature. She did start to feel she was doing a good job and Hannah began to turn into someone she could enjoy being with, rather than a huge source of worry.

Caring for your baby: feeding, sleeping and being held

The early relationship with your baby consists of three basic building blocks: feeding, sleeping and being held. In the early days the baby will probably do little more than sleep and wake for feeding with perhaps short periods of wakefulness. Sometimes it may feel as if the baby is always with you in the sense that even though he is asleep you do not feel separate from him or able to 'get back to normal' when he is asleep. This can make those initial days feel completely overwhelming and it may be difficult to do anything else other than attend to the baby.

Feeding the baby

You may be encouraged to feed your baby quite soon after his birth if he is wakeful and you are feeling fine. Most mothers will have decided during pregnancy whether they want to breast-feed or bottle-feed and many will keep an open mind to 'see how it goes' with breast-feeding.

Breast versus bottle

Recent years have seen an increase in numbers of women in this country breast-feeding, partly due to the efforts of Health Education programmes which highlight that nutritionally breast milk is the best food for babies. Breast-feeding confers health advantages for both baby and mother. Breast milk is easily digested, provides certain immunities for the baby and requires no sterilising or preparation. For mothers it reduces the risk of certain health problems later in life and certainly can help with weight reduction following pregnancy. In fact in recent times there are also attempts to encourage mothers to introduce solid food later and breast-feed exclusively for the first six months. However, a balance needs to be struck between what might be nutritionally best for a baby and what is best for parents. Probably very many women chose to bottle-feed because of the initial struggles with establishing feeding or because of a lack of support generally regarding feeding.

Breast-feeding

If you do decide to breast-feed, those first 48 hours are a critical time in terms of establishing some confidence about being able to breast-feed and not switching to bottle-feeding. During this time you are feeding your baby with colostrum and waiting for your milk to 'come in'. It may feel as if the baby wants to feed a great deal and it is this action in turn that will help to stimulate your milk production. Your milk 'arriving' can be extremely uncomfortable, often women wake to find their breasts enlarged and painful and this in turn can make it difficult for the baby to latch on. The basic task to be achieved in these first 48 hours or so is to get the baby into a comfortable position for feeding and to 'latch' him on correctly so that he is not sucking on the nipple alone. Breast-feeding is something that can only be learnt through experience and you will need your midwife to guide you initially to get the positioning established. The midwife will usually want feeding to be established before you leave the hospital and it is important to get as much help as possible while you are there.

Until you get the hang of breast-feeding, there may be a lot of anxiety for both parents. You may worry that the baby is not getting enough milk – this can be particularly acute if the baby was of low birth weight. There can be a number of difficulties initially with getting the baby into a comfortable position, which can in turn lead to sore nipples. Your breasts may become engorged as your milk comes in, making it difficult again to 'latch' the baby on.

More often than not, breast-feeding is shrouded in a Madonna and child image and the initial struggles are glossed over in order perhaps not to put women off. However, these initial problems are very common and perhaps if you are prepared for a rough-ride in the first few days you will be less likely to personalise the problems and feel it is because you aren't any good at it. The image of the breast-feeding mother does not convey the possibility of sore nipples, the mother still in bed at lunchtime because she has been feeding all morning or the endless fiddling around with pillows in order to get the baby into the 'right' position. It is at this point that the bottle can seem very attractive, particularly as you can see how much the baby has had. If breast-feeding seems not to be going well, all your fears about being a mother may resurface and you perhaps believe that the baby would be happier with the bottle. Here partners can be very supportive in terms of trying to just keep encouraging and acknowledging the difficulties. They should try to reassure rather than get carried away with the anxiety.

For some mothers breast-feeding seems to happen almost automatically or initial problems can disappear very rapidly. However, these first few days can seem like a lifetime and it can be difficult to remain positive. Many women move to bottle-feeding in this stage and it is important not to feel completely defeated if this is the case. To struggle on for too long may be hampering your relationship with the baby and your own ability to survive as a new mother. 'How long should I struggle with breast-feeding?' is a question that can only be resolved by you, your partner and the midwife.

It is not unusual for difficulties getting started with feeding to coincide with your being discharged from hospital. Usually midwives like to establish breast-feeding before you are discharged from hospital but often many other considerations overtake this decision. Although you may have been longing to get home to your own bed and away from other crying babies, it can feel difficult to get the help that you need at this stage. The community midwife does visit daily but this can seem like a lifetime to wait if your baby is not settling to feed. You may also find yourself with a houseful of smiling family visitors when you just want to be alone with the baby. It is important therefore to be assertive and get exactly what you need at this time. This is again an important role for the partner. He must be prepared to say 'no' to people, even to the doting grandparents, if that is going to hinder the mother's recovery.

'How often should I feed my baby?'

At this stage it is much too early to worry about whether or not you will feed your baby on demand (and we shall look at this in the next chapter), or any questions of how long and how much. You should feed your baby as often and for as long as he seems to want to. Your baby is learning too and as he learns and grows, his pattern will change as he manages to take in more milk. The newborn's stomach is about the size of a large walnut, so feeding has to be fairly frequent initially.

Feeding will be the focus of your early days with the baby. Almost all mothers seem to have worries about feeding at some point: is the baby getting enough milk? Is he putting on too much/too little weight? Should I start solids yet? It may be an anxious or difficult time now especially where you are recovering from a strenuous labour or struggling with sore nipples, but it is important to remember that all babies get enough to eat eventually and it takes time for feeding to establish. If things are going well, then try to relax and enjoy your baby: the action of being held and given nourishment in a relaxed way is an important aspect of your baby's emotional development.

Crying (the baby, not you!)

At this stage crying is really integral to feeding and sleeping. Newborn babies do not cry to manipulate you or annoy you or because they are bored. They are usually crying to signal the need for feeding. Sometimes they cry because of discomfort (perhaps they're wet) or possibly as a prelude to sleep but mostly it will be that they are hungry. In the next chapter the developing patterns of feeding and sleeping will be considered and questions such as whether or not we should pick up a crying baby or feed on demand. In the first few days of a baby's life it is important to learn about him and respond to him freely.

Babies do seem to be born with a temperament and some will appear to come out screaming whereas others will seem to be sleepy or 'easy to soothe'. Therefore from the first few hours of life, aspects of personality can already be seen. The 'temperament' of the baby is the beginnings of their personality. Psychologists have developed a number of ways of categorising people and one way developed by Thomas and Chess (1977) describes the early temperament of the child: 'the easy baby', 'the difficult baby' and the 'slow-to-warm-up baby'. The easy baby tends to develop feeding and sleeping cycles without too much trouble, is generally contented and reacts to new experiences without too much difficulty. The difficult baby is less easy to settle, reacts strongly to anything new and generally cries more. A third group are those who do not react strongly and tend to be more passive in their behaviour.

Although these may seem like generalisations as all children can behave in these different ways at different times, it is perhaps useful to consider that the way the baby behaves may affect how you feel about yourself as a mother. If your baby sleeps for the first 24 hours and you sleep and feel recovered, you may get off to a very positive start. If the baby is awake and crying a lot and you are exhausted, you may feel you don't really want to be a mother. Whether the child's early temperament is something fairly static or whether the child's personality is created in those early inter-actions is obviously a complex issue. The environment of the womb may have already contributed to early aspects of temperament, as may have the process of labour. What you need to remember at this stage is that the responses of the baby may not be what you expected and you need to give yourself time to get to know each other.

Returning to the issue of crying, therefore, the cries of the first few days while feeding is established are not necessarily predictive of later beha-viour and are also something that you are still getting used to. Research has shown that baby's cries are pitched at a frequency that gives maximum discomfort to the human ear. Clearly there is an evolutionary purpose to making sure that the baby's cries are heard and that he gets fed and looked after. Your baby's cries have evolved over thousands of years in order to make you respond. That is what you need to do in these first few days. In the next chapter we will consider how behaviours such as crying start to change in their meaning. In the later weeks babies may develop more persistent crying known as colic.

Sleeping

More likely than not your baby will spend an awful lot of time sleeping. However, those first couple of days may be affected by the labour and the baby may be particularly wakeful or particularly sleepy. At this stage it is important to concentrate on your own sleeping too. The baby has no concept of day or night and will sleep and feed in short cycles of a couple of hours that will gradually lengthen. In the early days the baby may seem to be feeding all the time but this will settle into more of a pattern in the coming weeks as the baby becomes more skilled in his feeding and takes in more milk at one time and therefore sleeps for longer.

The task is for you to learn to adapt your own sleep pattern for these early days, trying to get some rest/sleep while the baby sleeps. It is tempting in those first few hours to spend the time the baby is asleep chatting with visitors, phoning relatives, admiring the baby and sorting yourself out. However, when night comes, the baby may be wakeful and suddenly you feel exhausted and on your own with this little bundle of demands! Sometimes mothers can be so overwhelmed with the feelings of responsibility for the baby that they are almost frightened to go to sleep and not watch the baby. Many mothers have admitted that while in hospital they worried that the baby might be stolen if they fell asleep or that it might be confused with another baby. Also common is to worry that they would sleep through its crying or that the baby might not wake to feed. Babies are programmed to get what they need and their cries are designed to wake you. What is more common is that you are woken by every little shuffle or noise the baby makes.

Despite the fact that babies sleep a lot in the early days, it can often feel, with a first baby, as if you never get a moment to yourself. You may find in the early days that it takes half of the day to get showered and dressed. Even when a baby is asleep, they still take up a lot of the attention of the new mother. Many mothers will say 'he hardly sleeps at all', which is partly related to this preoccupation with and sense of being overwhelmed by the care of the baby. Dylis Dawes, a psychoanalyst, refers to the baby's sleep as the first 'separation' between mother and baby (Dawes, 1985). Perhaps in those early days you may find it difficult to disengage from the baby when he is asleep. He still fills your thoughts and your actions are all to do with concerns about your baby. If this is the case, you will find it more difficult to have time for yourself as you feel that the baby is always with you. Often when mothers have a subsequent baby, they cannot believe how they found it so difficult and time-consuming to look after the first. This again is about the enormous life shift that the mother has to make in order to care for her baby.

Sleeping and feeding are very closely related in this early stage and just as feeding will have no pattern in these early days, nor will sleeping, and expecting a routine can lead to disappointment. Gradually, over time, the periods of sleep and wakefulness will lengthen and longer periods of sleep will take place at night but this happens over the next six months or so.

Babies requiring special care

What we have talked about above may be totally different where a baby needs special care or is born with disabilities or needing surgery. Where a

baby is born early or 'small-for-dates', it may be just a case of special monitoring or help with feeding or keeping warm. A Special Care Baby Unit
(SCBU) or Neonatal Intensive Care Unit (NICU) can seem a very frightening or intimidating place at first with all its equipment and medical
atmosphere. The staff, however, will encourage you to be with your baby
as much as possible and to try and hold or touch the baby and feed where
possible. You will need to get lots of information as every child's prognosis
is unique. This can be a very upsetting start to your baby's life and to your
life as a parent. Also for babies that are born very early or small-for-date, it
may take some time to assess whether they are catching up with their peers
or what the longer-term implications are.

Where a child is born with disabilities, a very long process of adaptation
begins. Often the nature of these problems can only be assessed over time.
Even where a child is born with a recognised syndrome such as Down's
Syndrome, there is a wide range of possibilities in terms of how that child
will develop and what level of independence he will attain. Other children
may be born without a clearly defined syndrome but early assessment of
reflexes and so forth may suggest that there will be developmental delay.
It is difficult at this stage to assess the extent of disability that may occur
which can make the process of coming to terms with this situation much
more difficult. In such situations a whole range of supportive services may
need to be put in place. There are usually voluntary organisations for
particular problems and disabilities where it may help to meet other
parents who are dealing with similar problems.

Again, where babies are born with medical complications or needing
surgery, it may be difficult in the short-term to assess the extent of the
problems. Parents will need information from professionals and also the
careful support of relatives and friends.

When your baby is 'different', it can be very difficult to get support from
other new mothers. It may be that you feel resentful of their complaints
and feel that they 'don't know how lucky they are'. Many people around
you may find it difficult to know what to say and may be nervous, for
example, about holding the baby or upsetting you. Here you may find
organisations that deal with similar problems useful so ask your midwife
or doctors for any information on them. Usually parents of children with
disabilities will go through a process of bereavement: a sadness for the loss
of the healthy child they were expecting. This process may take a very long
time particularly where the extent of a child's disability or illness is not
known. It may be that the loss is experienced at points where the child
does not achieve the milestones at the time of his peers. It is important as
a parent to look for support at a time when you need it. You may find that as

time goes on you will be expected to have accepted the situation but this process is unique for every family.

Sally and Georgia's story

Sally was referred to me for depression and I met her when her daughter Georgia was six. Sally had known quite early on that Georgia could not hear. She didn't have a lot of contact with other mothers, as a single parent she had always worked full-time. Perhaps too she had avoided mother and toddler groups because her daughter was 'different'. She really felt she had come to terms with her daughter's disability but it was the progression to school that seemed to bring everything crashing down for her. She had been told in the past that her daughter had learning disabilities also, but it was only when she went to school that Sally was really having to face this fact. She had told herself that a learning disability would mean that her daughter would not be able to learn to read and write. However, the lack of progress in areas of physical development such as being continent gradually made it more difficult for Sally not to face up to the extent of her daughter's special needs.

Discharge from hospital

A mother's stay in hospital has become shorter over recent years: women tend to be healthier, are less likely to have general anaesthetic, there is more pressure on hospital beds and perhaps women to want to remove themselves more quickly to a home setting where they will still be visited regularly by the midwife. This may all seem very positive but there is evidence that shorter stays in hospital can lead to a higher incidence of post-natal depression. That shouldn't make you determined to stay in hospital but it should encourage you to think carefully about what is right for you. In many cases this may be to get away from a noisy and institutional setting to your own home. For others it might mean some precious time away from other responsibilities, to have time to get to know your baby, sleep when he does and have your meals cooked for you.

The midwife will encourage you to stay in hospital until you have 'established feeding'. Before being discharged you will need to be seen by the ward doctor and the baby will need to be seen by the paediatrician. These two things in themselves can mean that it is a long time between you deciding that you want to go home and your eventual departure home.

The experience of new parents

The physical recovery of mothers

Considering the exhausting and strenuous nature of labour, the speed at which most mothers recover really is quite remarkable. More often than not mothers are able to sit and hold their baby and chat quite happily within a very short time of delivery. However, almost all women need some time to recover. Most first labours may have been fairly long, you may have missed a night's sleep and almost certainly will have missed meals. The labour itself may have involved drug and/or practical intervention. With increasing numbers of women having epidural anaesthesia, the effects of this take time to wear off. You may have a catheter and will need to be monitored to see that you can urinate normally again. There may have been assisted delivery of forceps or ventouse, which may mean you have a tear or an episiotomy and possibly bruising or swelling to go down. The stitching following a tear or cut may take quite some time to carry out and lead to discomfort in sitting for some days. You will also bleed for some time following the delivery, usually lessening but possibly lasting a number of weeks. Breast-feeding your baby initially causes tiny contractions of the womb, helping it to return to normal size. These initially may be painful and cause your bleeding to be heavier. Caesarean births are become much more common and may even be seen as an easier option than labouring. It shouldn't be forgotten, however, that you have had a significant surgical procedure and have a wound that will take some time to heal. Generally, women do recover well without complications but it should be remembered that you are recovering from surgery and you may feel more uncertain about how to lift and hold your baby in those early days.

Recovery in hospital and after discharge does tend to focus on physical outcomes: are your stitches healing? Has your womb reduced in size? Are your bowels and bladder functioning? For some women this process can take a very long time and residual physical problems can mean a woman doesn't feel she has recovered properly for a very long time. Your physical recovery can have an enormous impact on your ability to parent your baby: if you cannot sit down easily, if you have become anaemic or are struggling with sore nipples, then you will feel less able to cope with the practical and emotional demands of your baby. Consequently, it's important not to assume that what you are feeling is normal: check things out with your midwife and see if there are other solutions. You may need iron supplements for your anaemia, or to try a different position such as lying down to feed or you may need the midwife to help you with latching the baby onto the nipple.

The emotional recovery of the mother and father

A very wide range of feelings and experiences can be considered a 'normal' reaction to having a baby. For many parents there is an initial period of elation when they finally become a family and when they explore their new baby. For others the experience may be different: more uncertain or overwhelming particularly where there are any concerns over the health of the baby or the mother. The first couple of days can, however, be something of an emotional roller coaster with most new mums shedding a few tears at some point.

The first few hours may be a time when the anxieties of the pregnancy and about the labour are over and the new arrival is safe and well, bringing much relief. There may be feelings of elation about becoming a family and possibly a sense of achievement from having survived the labour and producing a healthy baby, especially if he seems fairly settled. More negative feelings often stem from problems that occurred in the labour, the emerging relationship with the baby and feelings of being overwhelmed by the responsibilities of becoming a parent. Sometimes too it can be difficult to accept things not being as you had expected: perhaps to do with labour, perhaps to do with your partner, the gender of the baby, the temperament of the baby or how close you do or don't feel to him.

It is probably misleading to separate out physical and psychological recovery since the two have such strong effects on each other. However, emotional recovery is part of all of the areas we have talked about: how well the baby is feeding, his patterns of sleeping and how easily he seems to settle. Emotional recovery from the labour itself may be very rapid for some women as it becomes lost in the new preoccupations of looking after the baby. However, for some the thoughts of the labour just do not go away and can be quite preoccupying in these early days. Sometimes these problems can be resolved simply by the mother (and father too where appropriate) being allowed to recount and discuss their feelings about what happened in labour and to get explanations from the professionals about why things happened as they did. Generally hospital settings do not facilitate this type of approach. You may be in a shared room with nowhere to talk privately and more than likely no one is particularly available to sit and talk with you. A recent government directive has recognised that all new mothers should be encouraged to 'debrief' but psychological work always needs the right time and the right place and therefore this may not always take place.

Whether you feel great or awful initially, this doesn't necessarily last. This can be emotionally a very turbulent time. Your initial high may disappear: suddenly the baby needs feeding or starts crying, physical discomfort may kick in as the effects of any drugs wear off. Your tiredness may suddenly overwhelm you just as the baby decides to wake up for feeding. Your partner and or visitors may have gone home for the night and you may find yourself left holding the baby and uncertain of what to do. This may be the first night you have spent in a hospital or away from your partner. The care and support of those around you are crucial at this time. In some non-western societies women are given much more space to get to know their new baby and learn to be a mother without having to return to the demands of the rest of her life.

How do new dads feel?

The stereotype of the role of the new father is that of informing the expectant relatives about the new arrival and then leaving the mother to recover while he 'wets the baby's head' with the well-wishers. Probably most partners today want to remain much more involved with the mother and baby than might have been true in the last century. However, the idea of acting as a buffer to the outside world does still remain important. The partner can therefore dissuade visitors if they are not wanted or contact them when support from them is needed. The partner can organise the situation for the return home or, if necessary, he can just stay supporting and encouraging the mother.

Of course, these issues concern the recovery of the mother. The new father too may be experiencing his own reactions to the labour or fears about being a father and what that means. He may feel very uncertain about holding the baby and avoid doing so if he feels that the mother is doing a good job or if she keeps telling him how to do it. He may have mixed feelings towards the baby too especially if the mother only has time for the baby. There is evidence that being present at birth increases likelihood of bonding with the baby, however, the father may also feel shocked and overwhelmed by what has happened.

So, to summarize, a range of reactions can take place over the first few days and are all part of recovering from labour and the negotiation of the early tasks of parenting. Sometimes, however, these early problems might be a reflection of more complex problems to follow.

'Baby blues', post-natal depression and post-partum psychosis: complicated reactions to having a baby

The types of reaction that we have talked about so far are not unusual reactions after having a baby. So when do these reactions mean something more or turn into something more serious? It is something of a dilemma whether or not to get into 'categorising' women's reactions to having a baby. Many would argue that all women experience a sense of loss of their former self and life and a deterioration of the quality of their relationship (where they are in one). So maybe all of these reactions should be thought of as post-natal sadness and all women should be ready to experience some difficult times. One of the reasons for making some distinctions is that different types of problem may need different types of solution. Post-natal depression has been shown to have far-reaching consequences for both the mother and her child so if we can prevent it from happening or alleviate it more quickly, then this has positive consequences for all of the family. When suffering from emotional distress people naturally have questions about what is happening to them. How long will this last? Should I be taking any medication? All these questions are difficult to answer but are somewhat easier if we try to draw definitions between different types of problem.

Therefore, it can be helpful to think of three types of reaction after having a baby that do need to be distinguished from each other. The first is 'baby blues', the second, is post-natal depression, and the third is post-partum or puerperal psychosis. Post-natal depression (PND) will be covered in the next chapter, as it would not be an appropriate way to describe someone's initial emotional response to having a baby. PND develops more gradually over time. Baby blues and puerperal psychosis are usually seen in those early days. In looking at the statistics it is clear that baby blues is extremely common, PND is experienced by about one in ten women and puerperal psychosis by only about one in every thousand new mothers.

Baby blues?

What is it?

'Baby blues' refers to a period of low or changeable mood occurring in the first or second week of having a baby. It is something of a dilemma as to whether to put baby blues in a section looking at complicated reactions to having a baby since it is really quite difficult to separate this from the normal feelings and reactions already talked about. Most women feel tearful, frustrated or overwhelmed at some point in those first couple of days. Baby blues isn't an illness or even a proper psychiatric diagnosis, it is simply a way that people have tried to describe unpleasant feelings that occur shortly after having a baby and tend to resolve in a few days.

How common is it?

Statistically it is very common and levels of 50–80 per cent of new mothers are said to experience baby blues (Kendell *et al.*, 1981). The reason for perhaps labelling baby blues is to differentiate between this and post-natal depression. Baby blues refers to those reactions that occur around the first week after having a baby and tend to disappear in a couple of days. If you are feeling sad and tearful in those first few days, you are not post-natally depressed but if there are issues generating these tears, then they need to be looked at carefully, otherwise this might be an indication that post-natal depression could develop.

What causes it?

Very often feeling tearful or anxious can be after a poor night's sleep or it often coincides with your milk 'coming in' (which can be painful and make feeding more difficult). You may be very emotionally fragile, laughing one moment and crying the next. Trivial matters may provoke an argument or there may be anxiety type symptoms such as confusion or forgetfulness. These reactions tend to be short-lived and after a couple of days or a good night's sleep, things settle down.

One of the reasons for trying to describe a syndrome is because researchers can then look to see what might be causing these problems. There is research to look at whether baby blues is hormonally generated, whether it is linked to certain types of personality or, for example, poor experiences in labour. Not surprisingly there is not one clear reason why this happens. Giving birth is such an all-encompassing experience; it can be physically and psychologically strenuous or sometimes traumatic, you have to learn to look after your baby, accept a totally new routine, deal with feeding anxieties and come to terms with a whole new identity. This process is obviously unique for every parent and consequently we should concentrate on the individual difficulties that the new mother is experiencing rather than looking for a single explanation.

Does it need treatment?

The fact that these experiences are not 'serious' in the medical sense does not mean they shouldn't be taken seriously. It is important for those around the mother to try to understand her particular concerns and problems. If this is a lack of sleep issue, then what can be done to help her catch a few more hours? If this is to do with anxieties about feeding, then perhaps more support from the midwife is needed. Or it may be that there is someone else such as a friend with children or one of the grandparents who can provide some perspective on the situation. Often women may fear that they are going mad. One woman confided to me that after two sleepless nights in hospital she kept seeing her (deceased) mother every time she closed her eyes to go to sleep. She had to ask the midwives to feed the baby that night so that she could recover. She was just very tired.

It is important that the partner makes the midwife aware if he is concerned about how the mother is feeling or behaving, since he is the better judge of the mother's reactions. The midwife may not have met the mother before and may not know that someone is 'not themselves'. These early problems may be the roots of longer-term difficulties if not dealt with now.

Davina's story

Davina and Mike had been very excited about the arrival of their baby, which they had planned to have at home. Davina had been healthy throughout pregnancy and in her job as a solicitor was used to being in control of what was happening to her. She had read a lot about home births and felt prepared. Davina, however, did not go into labour spontaneously and eventually agreed to come into hospital to be induced. Despite a lot of pain and anguish Davina's labour did not progress and despite attempts to speed up the contractions after 24 hours the baby became distressed and had to be delivered by Caesarean section. Davina and Mike were delighted that they had a healthy baby girl and things seemed to go well initially with feeding. On her last day in hospital Davina waited all day to see the paediatrician and Mike eventually left to buy some food for their return home. When Mike returned Davina was in floods of tears and had apparently told the midwife that she wanted to discharge herself. She refused to wait to see the paediatrician and Mike was concerned that he shouldn't take her home in this emotional condition. They did go home but Davina did not feel better, becoming concerned then that the baby had not been seen by a doctor and was now crying and difficult to settle. Eventually Mike had to call out the GP and after a reassuring visit from him, Davina went to bed and woke feeling much happier. In the next few weeks they were both able to reflect on the stresses and disappointments that had led to Davina's tears.

Puerperal or post-partum psychosis

Very few books on pregnancy and childbirth will have a section on puerperal psychosis. This is possibly because it is so rare, affecting only around 1–2 mothers in every thousand. Probably there is a feeling that discussing it might frighten prospective mothers unnecessarily. There used to be a similar attitude to post-natal depression: that it was best not mentioned to mothers. This leaves problems somewhat shrouded in mystery and women who do have these problems are left to feel shameful about what has happened.

So what is puerperal psychosis?

Again, this is a condition that usually develops very rapidly after the baby is born. It may initially look like just the normal emotional struggles after having a baby. The mother may seem very anxious or agitated or tearful but, rather than subsiding, usually these symptoms escalate very rapidly. There are many different ways that these problems may present but quite quickly it becomes clear to those around the mother that her mental state is quite severely affected. What may start off as a fairly trivial anxiety about the baby may rapidly develop into an unshakeable delusion. For example, an initial concern about the baby's features may develop into an idea that the baby is a devil. The symptoms can be very varied but usually there is an initial 'manic' or excitable phase. The mother's ideas may be racing, her behaviour may be very hurried and inappropriate, for example, she may pick up the baby in a way that alarms those around her. (Almost all new parents worry about how to hold a baby but if you watch them picking him up, they will do it with great caution, adjusting their position in response to the baby or to the advice of others.) Her speech may be rapid and full of confused ideas and contradictions. She may become extremely paranoid about those around her and feel that they wish her or the baby harm.

The term psychosis is used to describe illnesses that are made up of delusions, hallucinations and often extreme paranoia. The symptoms in puerperal psychoses tend to be like those of manic-depression and more rarely schizophrenia. Alternatively the mother may just present as very depressed and unresponsive. Again it is important to emphasise that puerperal psychosis is extremely rare. If the mother has a history of serious mental illness, then both staff and family may have been alerted to the possibility of these problems in pregnancy.

Clearly, this can be very upsetting for partners and relatives who just cannot understand what is happening. These symptoms may initially be seen as just baby blues but it is their failure to resolve and their escalation that should alert everyone to their seriousness.

What causes it?

There is not really space in this book to cover this issue in depth. Like most psychological problems, a combination of genetic, biological, environmental and social factors has been studied. It is worth emphasising again that these types of illness are extremely rare. Also there are different factors involved depending on whether this is the first time that you have been ill or whether you have a history of (psychotic) mental illness. Where a woman has a history of manic-depression or schizophrenia she is more at risk for developing these problems. However, it is more likely that under these circumstances your doctors will monitor your pregnancy more closely and it may be that medical treatment is commenced shortly after the baby is born in order to prevent puerperal psychosis taking place.

How is it treated?

Puerperal psychosis needs immediate psychiatric intervention. Women will usually need to go into hospital to be assessed and monitored. They will usually need drug treatment and intensive support around caring for the baby. The relatives too will need support and information. A GP or a visit from the community midwife cannot provide this level of support. Because the presentation of post-partum psychosis is so dramatic, usually the services respond very quickly. Often the problems develop before the mother has left hospital, within hours of the birth.

What about the future?

The two main questions that parents have following these experiences are: How long will it take to recover? And, will it happen again if we have more children? To answer these questions a distinction needs to be made as to whether this is the first illness or a recurrence of previous problems.

Recovery for women with a post-natal psychosis is generally better than for someone experiencing a non-birth-related psychotic illness. However, hospital admissions will run into a number of weeks or months. The prognosis is better where you have only had a psychosis once following childbirth and you have no family history of similar psychiatric problems. With regard to further problems, there is probably around a 1-in-5 chance of this happening again in subsequent pregnancies and the risk is higher if you have had a psychotic illness before. For all women, however, careful support and monitoring are recommended around any future pregnancies.

Tara and Des's story

In the hours after her baby was born Tara became increasingly worried about the behaviour of the senior midwife and realised that this woman 'wanted to take her baby away from her'. She said nothing more while in hospital. Although Tara's partner was worried about her silence, he thought 'things would be OK' when they got home. Quite quickly Tara became convinced that a number of people were trying to steal her baby, including her own father. Tara locked herself and her baby into the bathroom and refused to come out or let anyone else in. After five hours of agonising Des broke the door in and eventually he convinced Tara that they should return to the maternity ward where the baby would be safe. From here Tara was admitted to a mother and baby unit. Her memory of the subsequent weeks was hazy but she made a full recovery.

I worked with Tara after the birth of her second child where she again became convinced that someone might try to take her child away. She told me that she knew whom to fear because they would say certain code words to communicate with each other and this 'gave them away'. She also told me that as a teenager following the death of her mother she had been tormented by strangers at night who tapped on her bedroom window. However, her fears were much less dramatic this time and she had not needed medication or hospital admission. Although Tara was unwilling to be dissuaded of her view that certain people wanted to take her children away, she was able to recognise that her 'protectiveness' was in itself, damaging for the children and gradually she began to let them have more freedom. She let them play with other toddlers and she started to mix with other mothers at a group for women with mental health problems. Here she felt a lot of support from other women, many of whom had also struggled with severe emotional problems while becoming a parent.

Those first few days!

So it is clear that those first few days can be quite a roller coaster of emotions and events. This is probably the biggest transition of most people's lives. For some it will be a wonderful time and hampered by few troubles. For most it will be an enormous upheaval but a rewarding one. For a very few it will signify a new and difficult time or the return of previous problems. Those first few days can seem like a lifetime and our next journey is through the first few weeks.

Who can help?

If you have your baby in hospital you will have access to both doctors and midwives to support you in those early days. Doctors will be particularly concerned with the medical aspects of your recovery and with the general health of the baby. Where you are recovering well, you may have little contact with the doctor. If you have any questions or concerns about your labour or about the well-being of your baby, then you may need to say that you want to speak to a doctor. The midwives will take the main role in supporting you in caring for your baby and particularly in helping you to negotiate the early stages of feeding your baby.

If you have your baby at home or after your discharge from hospital, you will be supported by the community midwife. The midwife usually visits daily but will be guided by what you need. Sometimes she may want to call when you are about to feed in order to assess any problems you may be having. The midwife can stay involved for up to 28 days but may sign off with the arrival of the health visitor if all is well.

The health visitor does a 'New birth visit' about two weeks after the baby is born and will be involved with your family until your child goes to school. Initially you will probably be visited at home. The health visitor will want to get to know you and find out about your birth and how you are coping with the new baby. If all is well, the health visitor will then encourage you to attend a baby clinic when you need to get the baby weighed or to discuss any specific concerns that you have.

Any problems either to do with the baby or your own physical or emotional well-being should be directed towards the midwife, health visitor or GP. Many health visitors and midwives are trained in counselling skills and will be able to support you with the emotional issues of this time. However, for a more serious problem, such as puerperal psychosis, an urgent psychiatric assessment is needed. The hospital or your GP can set this in motion. Services vary from area to area but many districts have special 'mother and baby' units for women with psychotic problems.

Discussion points

1. What sort of help might you need in the first few days? Do you want a relative or friend to stay with you or to visit and cook a meal? Do you want to be left alone, with no visitors, for the first few days until you find your feet?
2. How long do you think you might stay in hospital? What are your feelings generally about being in hospital? What previous experiences, if any, do you have of being in hospital?
3. What things can you arrange to make those first few days easier? Time off work for your partner? Someone to do some shopping?
4. What are your initial thoughts about your baby? Whom do you think he looks like or 'takes after'?

7

The first six weeks

In the first six weeks of a baby's life he will grow and mature rapidly. He will begin to feed for longer periods and you may be able to identify a pattern to his sleeping. There is, however, enormous variation: some lucky parents will have a baby that now sleeps through the night but for most there is still a great deal of variability in the feeding and sleeping cycles.

This is when the majority of new mothers will begin to 'settle into' parenting and grow in confidence as a mother. Even though the baby may not have developed any routines, you may have established some for yourself: about how you manage your life around the baby's needs. This is also a time when a small but significant number of women will start to show signs of not coping and around 10 per cent of women will have become depressed by the end of these first few weeks.

In this chapter the areas of feeding, sleeping and crying will be revisited to look at questions such as 'Should I feed a baby on demand?' and 'What is colic?' The development and capabilities of the baby will be considered also. Finally, the area of emotional recovery will be explored with particular attention given to post-natal depression.

The previous chapter highlighted some of the issues relevant to caring for your baby in the first few days. So, what are the tasks of the first six weeks? This is a time still largely dominated by feeding and sleeping (and crying) and, to an increasing extent, interacting. It is a time when the mother may find herself doing little more than feeding, trying to sleep and crying!

Feeding your baby

In those first few days you will probably have established whether you will breast-feed or bottle-feed and over the first six weeks feeding will become more firmly established if not perhaps as predictable as you might have hoped or expected. Quite quickly, as the baby grows, he will be able to take in more milk at one time and therefore he may sleep for longer or be able to go for longer periods between feeds. By six weeks the baby may sleep through the night or may wake two or three times to feed. The baby is probably feeding six or seven times in a day and sleeping in total for around 16 hours a day. Feeding initially mainly fills the baby's wakeful periods but gradually the baby becomes more alert and is beginning to explore his environment.

Feeding on demand

Fifty years ago you would have been encouraged to feed your baby every four hours or so and bottle-feeding was seen as a positive aspect of this regime. Breast milk is digested more quickly than formula and therefore 4-hour feeding must have been much easier for those bottle-feeding. The thinking behind this was that your baby needed to learn to wait and crying should not necessarily be seen as a signal that your baby needed feeding. In the 1970s and 1980s these ideas were swept aside and replaced by the belief that babies should be fed 'on demand' for however long they needed. These trends seem to reflect a more general feeling about who should take the lead when caring for children. Should the child's needs and wishes dominate the parent or the parent's dominate the child? You will be encouraged initially by your midwife to feed the baby whenever he seems to want to. This is because the baby cannot take in much milk initially and because it helps to establish your milk supply. However, you may find over the first six weeks that you want to begin to establish some sorts of feeding and sleeping routines so that you can plan your day. This is particularly important if you have other responsibilities: if you have to pick up a child from school at 3.30 p.m., you can't feed the baby at the same time.

Currently the pendulum seems to be swinging again away from total demand feeding with the idea that, even when breast-feeding it is possible, to introduce some sorts of pattern or routine and not just feed the baby every time he cries or puts his head up to the breast. Perhaps in a climate where women want to return to work and also to have time for their own needs, the concept of letting the baby dictate has become more unworkable. Also for the mother who is struggling with becoming a parent, the idea of imposing some structure must be very appealing. Currently the best-selling book for new parents is *The New Contented Little Baby Book* (Ford, 2002). This recommends a routine for feeding and sleeping right from birth and its success perhaps reflects a shift away from demand feeding. So how are mothers supposed to decide what is right?

In the early days with your baby, the midwife will encourage you to feed whenever the baby seems to want to, especially if you are breast-feeding as this will help your milk supply to become established. After this, it is up to you, and for many mothers it is something that just evolves without them having decided from the start. It is important to remember that the baby is involved in this decision too. He may quite quickly settle into having long sleeps and feed well at each sitting and therefore be able to go for quite long periods. It may be easy therefore to establish a pattern of 3- or 4-hourly feeding with a long sleep at night. However, many babies seem to want to feed almost constantly at times and there may be days when they seem particularly hungry. Probably if your baby wants to feed a great deal, you will be trying to encourage him to go for longer so that you can get out of the house occasionally! However, if you are determined to set some sort of routine, you may have to put up with your baby not liking it and expressing his displeasure.

Again, it is important to respond to your baby and not to expect him to be the same as your friend's baby. There is enormous variation in what babies do: if your baby doesn't feed very often or feeds continually, this is still considered normal. It may cause you problems if your baby wakes frequently at night but it only makes your stress greater if you persecute yourself with self-doubt about your competency as a mother. Just because someone else's baby sleeps through the night doesn't mean that they have necessarily done anything different from you.

Probably by the end of the first six weeks most mothers are feeling reasonably content about feeding their baby, that he is growing and that life is settling into some sort of pattern. Usually with babies, as soon as you have deciphered some sort of pattern, it changes. You are feeding at regular intervals then suddenly the baby wants to feed all day again – probably he is having a growth spurt. Alternatively he may catch a cold and seem sleepier and less interested in feeding. By the time these events have passed, the baby will have grown and changed and his routine may now be completely different from before.

As was mentioned in the last chapter, feeding a baby or an infant seems to be a source of anxiety for most parents at some point. It may be concerns about whether he is gaining weight or getting enough milk as an infant. Later on there can be difficulties around introducing solids: when, how much, what he will or won't eat? With toddlers there may be times when they appear to eat next to nothing for weeks, they may refuse fruit and vegetables or eat only a small range of foods. Only a tiny proportion of children have a 'failure to thrive' resulting from a problem around feeding. The vast majority of parents, however, will have at least one period of concern about their children's eating, many are still worrying after their children have left home. Perhaps we have an almost instinctive preoccupation with feeding since it is only in recent years and in the western world that most of us are free from genuine concerns about our children having enough to eat.

Crying

As discussed in the last chapter, babies are highly adept at getting their needs met, and crying is an important part of signalling what they need. At this age crying is still usually a signal that the baby wants feeding. However, crying may increase over the first six weeks and some babies develop what is known as 'infant colic'. Colic refers to periods of intense crying that seems to continue despite attempts at feeding, holding or rocking. This often occurs in the early evening or is at its worst at this time. It can begin in the first few weeks of life but seems to resolve spontaneously after a couple of months. That might not seem long with hindsight but, at the time, it can be incredibly distressing and stressful for the mother and father. Early evening is often a time when other responsibilities kick in such as preparing a meal or putting other children to bed. It is also when the mother may feel most tired and her milk supply may be at its lowest, possibly exacerbating the problem.

Although references to infant colic have been around since the ancient Greeks, the reason for it remains elusive. Many physical and psychological hypotheses have been explored. The physical causes can be grouped into immaturity of the gastrointestinal system, cow's milk intolerance, intolerance from foods being eaten by the mother and passed via the breast milk or immaturity of the central nervous system. From a psychological perspective there have been suggestions of difficult infant temperament, parent−infant interaction problems or a 'hyper-sensitivity' in the baby so that any interaction, for example, holding or dressing the baby, leads to crying. The fact that the crying resolves at three or four months of age without any intervention makes some of these explanations seem unlikely.

With regard to the interaction difficulties, there is no consideration of cause and effect: it seems very likely that parents become more anxious in their interactions if their baby is crying a lot for no apparent reason. In fact, research has shown that the mothers of infants with colic are prone to more feelings of anxiety, depression and inadequacy. However, considering that their babies are crying inconsolably, it would seem more worrying if these mothers weren't showing any signs of distress!

In the absence of any reliable explanation of infant colic, it seems important to think more about how to survive it until it resolves rather than how to 'cure' the colic itself. There are other sources of advice on infant colic but before trying out any 'natural' remedies it is always important to check this out with your GP or health visitor.

Managing infant colic

- Try to adapt your evening routine so that one parent is free to manage the baby. If you are on your own, try to get a relative or friend to come around to hold the baby and give you a break.
- Find things that soothe the baby generally, perhaps a trip out in the car or pram, if that is at all possible at that time of the day. Maybe a bath or playing him some music will help. These things are very individual and some babies may become more distressed by further stimulation.
- Try to free yourself from the stress of the situation. Get as much support as you can. It may feel difficult to keep asking a relative or friend to come around and 'hold the baby' but remember this won't go on forever. Remember too that other people will find the cries of your baby less distressing and therefore easier to deal with. For a mother the cries of her own baby stir up very primitive emotions, for others they are just the sounds of a baby crying. Also you have been dealing with the baby all day and all night too probably, so allow yourself to take some support if it is available.
- Alongside this, try not to allow yourself to become demoralised by the babies crying. Infant colic will resolve itself, no matter what you do. Blaming yourself and thinking it is because you are a useless mother will only make you feel worse and less able to cope with a situation that is very emotionally demanding.
- There are self-help organisations that may be able to offer support and advice. Usually on a telephone help line you will be able to talk to another parent who has experienced similar problems (see list of addresses of organisations that can help on p. 181).

Most babies do respond to being picked up and talked to or sung to. However, many mothers have been told, perhaps by their own mothers, that picking up a baby too much will spoil him and make him cry even more. Is it such an awful thing to pick up a crying baby or are we just 'making a rod for our own back'? There is research to show that attending to babies' cries quickly actually decreases the amount of crying in the first three months. It is a decision really about what you want your baby to learn: 'don't bother crying because it makes no difference to how I behave' or 'if you need something, then let me know'. Sometimes, if you are really struggling to cope, then you may have to put your baby down safely somewhere and let him cry while you take some moments away from the situation to calm down. However, routinely leaving a baby of this age to cry in his cot is not a good idea, babies can very easily become overheated and all that crying may mean he needs milk again more quickly.

Annabelle and Hugh's story

Annabelle came to see me when her second child was six weeks old. She came as an urgent referral as the GP said she was 'absolutely beside herself with worry' about her son Harry. Annabelle told me that Harry was in terrible pain most of the time, crying and 'pulling his legs up to his tummy'. Harry had seen many doctors including the consultant paediatrician and all had concluded that her baby had 'colic'. Annabelle found this particularly difficult to accept as she had not had similar problems with her first baby and she deeply resented the suggestion that she was an anxious mother. In the course of our discussion it became clear that she was feeling very unsupported by Hugh who had a very busy job as a barrister and whom she said she hardly ever saw. She suspected that he might be having an affair and she resented the number of nights that he stayed late at work.

Harry's colic gradually disappeared over the next few weeks and Annabelle said she had been exhausted and distraught with the stress of dealing with the crying. With hindsight she didn't really think that Hugh was having an affair, she simply resented his time spent away from the home. Once Harry had improved, she felt she could cope generally and that she would just have to come to terms with Hugh's commitment to his job. Hugh was unable to come to the session that I had invited him to attend.

Sleeping

Within the first six weeks of your baby's life his pattern of sleeping may be very unpredictable. Gradually through the course of the first year of life his sleep will become more concentrated in the night-time and his periods of wakefulness during the day will increase. There is a great deal of variability between babies about how long they sleep at any one time. This is also clearly linked to feeding. As the size of the baby's stomach grows and as his feeding abilities increase, he will take in more milk and be able to sleep for longer periods. Some babies may sleep for three or four hours at a time during the day, others will be awake again after half-an-hour.

The fact that your baby wakes during the night is clearly a 'problem' for parents as it disturbs their sleep and generally makes life harder during the day. However, health professionals will not be keen to diagnose your child as having a sleep problem before they are at least six months of age. This is mainly because night-time waking in the first six months is extremely likely but it is also because any intervention targeted at a child younger than six months is unlikely to be successful or, if it is, the results may be short-lived. Babies in the first couple of months will be waking because they are hungry and because they have completed a sleep cycle. Achieving your baby 'sleeping through the night' can become a great preoccupation but it isn't the whole story. Most parents, at different stages throughout the first few years of your child's life, will have to deal with settling problems or night-time waking. Teething, coughs and colds, changes in daytime routine, daytime sleeping: there are many things that can lead to night-time interruptions.

Coping with interrupted nights

If you are finding it particularly difficult in the night, perhaps you could try some of the following:

- If you can, express some milk and get your partner to take one of the night feeds.
- If you are bottle-feeding, you could share the feeding so that one of you does late nights and one does the early mornings.
- Try to sleep while your baby is sleeping. If your baby only sleeps in short bursts, then this may be unrealistic, as you can feel worse if you are woken again after 30 minutes. Alternatively, perhaps you can get someone to 'watch' the baby while you get some sleep during the day.

- If the baby is wakeful in the evening, ask your partner to 'hold the baby' while you get some sleep. Try to work out some sort of timetable so that you can both get sufficient sleep to manage the feeding.
- Most professionals who work with babies will recommend that you try to put your baby down to sleep while he is still awake, rather than rocking him or letting him fall asleep in your arms. This is so that your baby will be able to settle himself to sleep when he wakes from a sleep cycle at night rather than having to have you there. This is an issue to discuss with your health visitor and, like demand feeding, is a choice to be made by the parent. Many mothers may feel that this spoils their contact with their baby and they enjoy him falling asleep while feeding or being cuddled.

Is it OK for the baby to sleep in our bed?

Another issue linked to the sleeping patterns of babies is where your baby should sleep. Co-sleeping, or the baby sharing the parental bed, seems to be a growing trend in recent years and we perhaps imagine that this is a modern invention. However, for thousands of years infants have slept with their mothers and this is still very much the norm in many non-Western societies today. In fact, in some societies women think it almost neglectful for infants to sleep separately. However, we cannot necessarily compare these situations and assume that it is therefore safe. Our ancestors didn't sleep on mattresses, under duvets and in centrally heated houses.

The issue of co-sleeping has also become linked with the issue of 'cot death' or Sudden Infant Death Syndrome (SIDS). Since a directive in the last few years that babies should sleep on their backs, the rates of SIDS has dropped dramatically. The Foundation for the Study of Infant Death provides very good information about decreasing the risk of SIDS. Their address is given in the list of addresses on p. 181 and they have a very accessible website (www.sids.org.uk).

Clearly, certain sleep environments are more risky for babies. There has been research to suggest that co-sleeping might in fact be preventive in SIDS since co-sleeping causes a different level of arousal in babies. Having your baby in the same room (in the early months) is also preventive perhaps for the same reasons. The relationship between SIDS and co-sleeping is complicated. A recent large population study identified certain risks to be avoided: co-sleeping on a sofa, co-sleeping after the recent consumption of alcohol, where you are extremely tired, the infant being under a duvet and parental smoking (Blair *et al.*, 1999).

Interacting, exploring and learning

Feeding initially fills most of the baby's wakeful periods but gradually the baby becomes more alert and is beginning to explore his environment. His tiny movements seem totally random but are in fact tiny steps in his development. As mentioned in the previous chapter, from a very early age your baby is able to recognise your face and your voice. Attachment is a two-way process and the baby is primed to develop a relationship with someone who will love and take care of him. One of the first things a baby learns to do is to make eye contact and then to imitate facial gestures. If you hold your face close to your baby's and open your eyes and mouth widely as if surprised, an awake and alert baby will try to copy you (see Murray and Andrews, 2000, for amazing photographic evidence of newborn babies' capabilities). Also in the first six weeks, you will probably see the first social smile: babies will get their features into a 'smile' from birth but this is different from a smile that was intended. A smile will eventually be elicited by the approach of, or interaction with, the mother or father. Increasingly the baby will be soothed by a familiar voice and will begin to make sounds in response to the parents' talk. The baby will also be soothed by being picked up or held.

Communication between mother and baby does not begin when your baby starts to 'babble' or says his first words; communication begins from birth in these interactions. It has also been argued that the turn taking that is necessary for communication in speech begins during feeding. Careful analysis of mothers and babies during feeding has shown that there is a 'burst–pause' cycle (Kaye, 1982). Basically, this means the baby feeds, then stops, before feeding again. Mothers will spontaneously 'jiggle' the baby during the pause and he will begin to feed again. A pattern develops so that the baby responds to the mother's encouragement to continue. Mother and baby are 'communicating' with each other about the feeding.

In the past, parents would not have been encouraged to communicate with babies as it was assumed that they just fed and slept in a rather mechanical way. However, psychological research evidence from the past 30 years shows that even from a very early age there is *reciprocity* between mother and baby. This responding to each other, which goes on without us even really noticing, seems to be central to how babies learn and develop in these early months. This is possibly too where early difficulties in feeding and with crying begin. Where mothers are very anxious or very depressed, they fail to respond to cues from the baby that he is hungry, tired or uncomfortable. Consequently, the baby may cry more as he is not eliciting the response that he needs.

It seems important therefore to continue the dialogue that began back in pregnancy. It is important to try and relax and listen to and be guided by the baby. Both parents should feel free to hold, look at, talk to and listen to their baby. Previous generations may have believed that you 'spoil' a baby by picking him up too much but, in the long term, the more you know and understand your baby, the easier it will be to negotiate his infancy. This doesn't necessarily mean your life has to be totally dominated by the baby: if he learns that you 'usually' respond quickly, then he will be able to tolerate a little frustration. If you only respond after he has cried for 20 minutes, then he will learn that this is what he needs to do to get your attention.

Your baby will grow and develop rapidly over the next few weeks and months. A baby's development will often be talked about in terms of achieving his 'milestones': such as lifting his head, sitting unaided, crawling or taking his first steps. Clearly, for all babies these have to happen in a certain sequence: you cannot walk before you can sit up. However, there is a wide age range at which these milestones will be achieved. Right from birth, however, your baby will be weighed and measured and his progress on these measurements can be a source of anxiety or disappointment for a parent. Mothers will often leave the baby clinic proudly announcing their baby's weight (which really doesn't mean a lot to you unless you have a baby of a similar age) and this can be very difficult for a mother who has a baby that is not gaining lots of weight or later a child that seems to be developing at a different rate to his peers. These differences are usually insignificant in the long term, so it is important to try not to become too caught up in comparing your baby to others.

Changing relationships

As discussed in Chapter 3, now there are new social roles to be learnt by all members of the family. By six weeks you are probably getting used to the idea of yourself as a mother or father, even if only in terms of getting used to people using the term in relation to you. This learning carries on throughout your child's life. A new baby can lead to unexpected reactions in others. You may find your own parents a great source of help and support or you may be disappointed by their lack of involvement or their over-bearing advice. Perhaps it's important to remember that they are learning too and that you may find it very useful in the future to have help and support from family members even if it involves some costs.

Often there may be disappointments or disagreements about the sharing out of tasks within the home. Sometimes post-natal emotional problems have their roots in dissatisfactions with the relationship between the couple. It is important to remember that you need to be explicit about the help that you need. Research has shown that where women asked for specific types of help, they got more support at home and their relationships improved. This may seem like stating the obvious, but in a situation that is new to everyone it is always important to keep talking about what you need.

Becoming a sibling

If this is not your first baby, then you will have an older child or children who must learn a new role as brother or sister. It can be a very difficult transition for children to come to terms with a new baby and their reactions can be very varied. They may 'regress' in their behaviour, for example, start wetting again once potty-trained, they may want to drink from a bottle, want to be carried all the time or to sleep in the parental bed. You may worry that your child will 'resent' the baby only to discover that your child loves his new sister but is constantly angry with you. However your child reacts, he needs your support and understanding. Try to involve him with the new baby and to spend a little time, perhaps while the baby is sleeping, doing something just with him. Often your child may strengthen his relationship with his father or a grandparent at this time, so that he has a special person to be with when your attention is taken up with the new arrival.

The recovery of the mother

Physical recovery: 'What happened to my pelvic floor?'

As the first six weeks progress women should start to feel much better physically. Usually any bleeding will have stopped or lessened considerably, stitches should have healed and women post-Caesarean should be feeling that their wound has healed. Of course many women do have complications and prolonged healing and any concerns should be raised at the 'six week check'. This is an appointment that you will have with your GP to discuss your health and well-being. It is important to get help with any concerns that you have rather than just hoping they will go away.

When you are discharged from hospital, you will probably be given some information on your health post-natally such as exercises for getting back into shape or how to improve the muscles in your pelvic floor. If this is not the case, then try to speak to your midwife, health visitor or GP if you have any concerns. For example, some women go on to have problems with stress incontinence following physical trauma in labour. This can be prevented by exercise of the pelvic floor muscles.

The emotional journey continues

Psychologically, most women feel that the first six weeks are an extreme and intense time emotionally. An enormous shift has occurred from the day that the baby was born to this point where the majority of parents are feeling a sense of life settling down to some sort of normality. That 'normality' might mean a baby that is totally unpredictable and a great deal of uncertainty but it is more the sense that you are coping with this new life, if still at the beginnings of it.

However, six weeks seems to be a peak time for women to start showing signs of depression. Around 10 per cent of new mothers could be diagnosed as depressed at this time. In some areas of high social deprivation, the figure is considerably higher (unpublished figures from my own work in an inner London area show levels as high as 25 per cent). This probably reflects the greater number of pressures that these women/families have to cope with. However, it shouldn't be thought that middle-class families do not experience post-natal emotional problems: post-natal depression is common across all social groups and can affect anyone. That is not to say, however, that it is something that we have to be victim to, an 'illness' that we just suffer and can do nothing about. Research has shown that there are ways of reducing the levels of emotional problems in new mothers both by preventing them from happening and by supporting mothers and families when they occur.

What is post-natal depression?

As has been emphasised, all women have good and bad days when they are getting used to being a mother. The lack of sleep that many mothers experience would be enough to make most people feel fed-up or tearful. Most new mothers will feel at times that they are not making a good job of parenting or feel sad about the things that they would like to do and can't. Depression, however, is something different to this, something deeper, more persistent and debilitating.

What does it feel like?

In terms of symptoms, post-natal depression (PND) may be experienced in a number of different ways but characterised by the persistent low mood that is common to depression at any time. The most common symptom is to feel tearful and easily upset. For other women it may be irritability and mood changes that are troubling them. Often these emotions are linked to how the new mother is feeling about herself as a mother: she may lack confidence, feel useless and compare herself negatively to others. In Chapter 4, the 'biological' symptoms of depression were highlighted and these are common in PND: changes in appetite, sleep problems and lack of energy, poor concentration and feeling unable to cope with the care of the baby and the usual daily tasks. Clearly, in the early days, after having a baby some of these problems can be mistaken for just the normal struggles of having a new baby. I have seen many women who have terrible sleep problems but attribute it all to 'getting up to the baby'. Lying awake at five in the morning worrying about coping is not the same as waking to feed the baby. Depression after giving birth is often masked as tiredness or 'Well, everybody gets a bit tearful when they have just had a baby.'

Often post-natal sadness manifests itself as extreme anxiety, particularly about the baby or about some aspect of the birth or the mother's labour or recovery. Jenny, whose story was in the last chapter, became preoccupied with Hannah's milk intake to the detriment of everything else. Clearly, for many women these issues are very real but if you become preoccupied with your labour difficulties to a point where you can't get on with your life with the baby, then perhaps there are problems to be looked at in more depth.

Is it different from depression at any other time?

Statistically, depression is fairly common for women: being at home/not working and looking after children are two strong 'risk factors' for developing depression. So is there anything different about 'post-natal' depression? Depression in the year following childbirth is fairly common but many young women of a similar age will also be depressed. However, women seem to be much more likely to get depressed at around six weeks after the birth of their baby, which does suggest that there are factors specific to those first few weeks that put you at risk for depression. As has been said, around 10 per cent of mothers will become depressed at this point but rates of depression do seem to peak again at points later in the first year, so it is probably easier to regard the whole of the first year as a time of risk for post-natal depression.

For many women it may be that they have a history of depression and this is simply another stressful time that triggers depression but for a distinct group of women this will be the first time that they have been depressed. Another factor that seems to be common with post-natal depression is that it is often not recognised. For many women it is only when they recover that they realise that they were depressed and that their experience was different to other women's. Some women maybe never identify that they were depressed, they simply shut out the experience and get on with their responsibilities. It is perhaps difficult to admit to being depressed when the world around you is just seeing the positive. It's great to come round and 'coo' over the baby for half-an-hour but very different when you are with this baby 24 hours a day.

Clare and Ian's story

Clare had worked as a nanny since leaving school, loved children and couldn't wait to start a family of her own. Her husband Ian was perhaps less enthusiastic but he wanted what Clare wanted. At 25 Clare gave birth to a baby boy, Edward, and initially all was well. She received a great deal of help from her mother and in fact often stayed overnight there as Ian was a shift-worker and Clare didn't like being alone with the baby. When Clare came for help, she did so extremely reluctantly. She initially said that she had just been having a bad day when she had seen the GP who referred her, and really she was fine. She said she had been tearful at the time because she was having terrible problems with breast-feeding. When she began to speak about this, she was instantly in floods of tears and remained so throughout our meeting. She had stopped breast-feeding because of an infection in her breast, which she perceived to be a terrible failure, especially as she had always felt critical of mothers who bottle-fed. She said her mother had encouraged her to bottle-feed from the start and now at least she could get her mother to do some night-time feeds. She had spent all of the last week at her mother's house and said she was worried about things with Ian because he and her mother just didn't get on. Ian didn't feel confident that they could manage the baby and accepted that it would be better if Clare stayed with her mother, especially while he was working. Clare rarely went out and found the idea of going

> *shopping or out in the car without her mother almost impossible. She said she rarely got dressed at all most days and said she wouldn't eat a thing if her mother weren't cooking for her.*
>
> *It took Clare many months to finally feel confident enough to look after her baby in her own home with Ian. Every time she got a bit better she would give herself a hard time about why she had been able to look after other people's children but was terrified of looking after her own baby.*

What causes post-natal depression?

As with depression at any point in the life cycle, there are a range of ideas about what causes PND, including biological factors, social and life factors and things to do with your psychological make-up. There seems to be a range of factors that might cause a woman to become depressed after having a baby and these factors are different for each new mother. The enormous physical and hormonal changes associated with pregnancy and childbirth may be a factor for some women. There are also genetic aspects to depression: if close relatives have suffered from depression, this makes your risks of experiencing it higher. Also if you have been depressed before, then the transition to parenthood may be another event that triggers depression.

The enormous social and life changes that occur when having a baby are probably the most significant factor: women have to assume the new role of a mother, saying goodbye to a child-free life and coming to terms with the responsibility of looking after someone else. This is obviously much more difficult where women are isolated and lack of support, have problems in their relationship and are struggling with other life issues such as unemployment, poverty and housing difficulties. There are also factors to do with your experience of the pregnancy and birth itself and a poor experience of labour, particularly in terms of it not meeting your expectations, can be a cause of depression. If you have had difficulties in your own childhood, particularly a poor relationship with your own mother, then this seems to increase your risk of becoming depressed.

No one factor or explanation seems to be enough to explain the occurrence of emotional problems following birth and perhaps the term 'post-natal depression' is just a label for similar symptoms caused by a wide range of different problems and experiences for different women. The stories below highlight some experiences of post-natal depression.

Post-natal depression and birth-related problems

Very many women find that at six weeks they have hardly recovered from the birth of the baby and aspects of their delivery may be holding back their recovery and it is not unusual for this to lead to depression. This may be particularly true where your baby is born pre-term, needs special care or is born with disabilities or health problems. The temperament of your baby may also prove challenging to you. If your baby has struggled with feeding and appears difficult to settle, then you are more vulnerable to feelings of inadequacy or confusion and this can slip into depression.

Fiona and David's story

Fiona and David had their first baby, Louisa, when Fiona was 37. They both worked for a merchant bank and Fiona was hoping to return to work as soon as she felt well enough, but definitely intended to do so within three months. Fiona's labour had started within a couple of days of her maternity leave beginning and she said she had been terrified when she had felt the first contraction. She said she had a feeling of being 'caught out' and 'unprepared' since she had been so focused on her job just a few days before. Her labour was long and had eventually to be speeded up with a drip as her contractions had slowed down. This intervention had caused her terrible pain she said and there had been too much delay in her getting an epidural. She blamed this delay for the fact that she needed a forceps delivery after many failed attempts at trying to push the baby out. Fiona said that she had felt like she had been battered with a cricket bat afterwards. She found her stitches terribly painful and she was plagued by cramping pains in her abdomen. Two weeks after Louisa was born, Fiona developed a bladder infection and was confined to bed with her mother having to come and help look after the baby. Eventually, she returned to hospital and it was discovered that there was retained placenta needing further intervention. After a course of antibiotics, she was feeling better but breastfeeding had broken down completely in this time.

By six weeks after the birth Fiona still felt she had not recovered and that her stitches were still painful. A phone call from her boss to discuss her plans for returning to work seemed to be the trigger for her depression as it emphasised for her just how much her experience had been different from her expectations.

Post-natal depression and echoes of the past?

Often we find ourselves drawn into repeating the patterns of our own childhood and where there were significant difficulties for our parents, particularly between them then this can cause difficulties for new parents both mothers and fathers. Having to care for a needy baby can stir up feelings of need in ourselves.

Karen and Colin's story

Karen was 16 when she had her first baby, Sophia. Colin already had two children from a previous relationship although he did not see them regularly as the relationship with his former partner was difficult. Karen struggled a great deal in those early weeks and felt totally overwhelmed at times by the baby waking at night and the constant feeding. She said that at times she thought Sophia would be better off 'in care', something she knew all about having spent many periods of her own childhood in care. She told me that sometimes she had to leave Sophia crying in the bedroom and put her head under a cushion, as she couldn't stand it. She had little contact with her own mother who had been totally against the pregnancy as she had seven children of her own and said she didn't want to end up bringing up Sophia. Colin initially was very supportive and helped out with feeding at night but after the first couple of weeks he said he was exhausted and took to spending long periods in bed. Often there was no food in the house either because there was no money or because neither Colin nor Karen felt able to get to a shop. Colin absolutely idolised his own father and had hoped to be as good as him. However, Colin tended to be preoccupied with his inability to provide materially for the children and would go to his own father to get money to buy the baby elaborate toys and designer clothes.

In time Karen began to recognise that both she and Colin were totally unprepared for having children and that she desperately needed more support with looking after the baby. She moved in with an older sister and her husband and gradually with help from her sister became more able to cope with the care of Sophia. Karen intended to return to Colin 'at some point' if he could sort himself out.

Post-natal depression and life events

As previously mentioned, many women experience a number of life issues and events either due to the pregnancy itself or with it. For some women the sheer number of difficulties that they have to manage seems to be what triggers their depression.

Hayley and Enrique's story

Hayley and Enrique were both pursuing careers in the entertainment industry. Hayley was a children's entertainer who hoped to break into children's television and Enrique was a drummer with a band. Enrique was often away on tour for long periods and with two uncertain incomes they had not planned their pregnancy. Despite all the obstacles and uncertainties they had begun to look forward to the birth of their baby. However late in the pregnancy Enrique had a chance to tour in the USA and they decided he should go as at least it offered some income. Just after Enrique's departure their landlord who was a 'friend' announced that he had sold their flat and wanted her out in the next month. Consequently, at 35 weeks pregnant, Hayley had to return to her mother's house 200 miles away. Hayley had to stay in the bedroom that she had had as a child and cope with her mother treating her like a 'naughty child' who had got herself into a terrible mess. Hayley's baby, Joel, was born at 37 weeks and spent the first week in Special Care as he was of low birth weight and needed monitoring. Hayley's original enthusiasm about the baby was completely crushed by the experience of the last days of her pregnancy. She deeply regretted having let Enrique go to the US, as after a short visit to see the baby he had to return. She felt that everything she had done had been the wrong decision. She was angry with Enrique, with her landlord and with her mother but at the same time felt she couldn't express it. Her mother was keeping a roof over her head and Enrique was trying to earn money. She felt trapped at her mother's house and although generally her mother was trying to help, she felt she couldn't stand to be with her and she spent a lot of time up in her bedroom feeling like she wanted to 'explode'. She also worried greatly about Joel who was gaining weight very slowly in the early months and she found the concerns of her GP and health visitor threatening as she was sure eventually Joel would be taken into care as she had proved herself 'such a useless mother'.

After a couple of months Enrique left the band and returned home. He found accommodation and Hayley joined him. Money was extremely tight but Hayley's parents did help out. Hayley said she had just become so miserable she couldn't get out of it. However, this was a turning point and gradually things improved. When Joel was a year or so old Hayley was beginning to enjoy her life again and she was reassured that Joel was 'fighting fit' now. She began to take some work doing children's parties as she had a friend who would look after Joel for an afternoon. It took time but gradually Hayley began to enjoy her new life.

Post-natal depression and support

Very often depression occurs after childbirth because the new mother is socially isolated: she may have few family and friends around her and may find herself alone at home with the baby for long periods of time. Depression is more common where there are relationship difficulties or the partner is frequently absent. Sometimes people may be unaware that a new mother is struggling as she is 'keeping up a brave face' for the outside world.

Sue and Stella's story

Sue had two children, Lauren and Josie, by donor insemination. Following her first pregnancy she recovered well and Stella, her partner, was keen for them to try again for another pregnancy. They knew they could only have a small number of attempts at this treatment as they wished their daughter to have a biological sibling (and therefore they were limited by the donor supply). As Sue was in her early forties, they felt they should 'get on with it' and on the second attempt Sue became pregnant and had a second daughter. After this roller coaster of events Sue realised that the world would expect her to be blissfully happy: from an unlikely situation she had managed to have two beautiful children. However, the day-to-day reality of her life was, she said, a nightmare. Lauren, her eldest daughter, still woke regularly at night and came into their bed for the duration. Josie was feeding often at night and seemed to sleep very little during the day. Sue said she felt her age at times and although she loved the girls totally, she desperately hated the monotony of the days. Stella worked as a journalist on a Sunday newspaper and spent less and less time at home as the week progressed. Sue had little real support with the children. Both sets of parents lived at a distance and Stella's family still could not accept that she had not married a man and had a family.

Sue had very little support through these difficult times. She had avoided ante-natal classes and mother and baby groups because she felt she might have to keep explaining her 'situation' to others. She found little in common with her friends as they either had older children or had not had a family. Everyone assumed that she was happy which made it more difficult for Sue to admit that she wasn't enjoying being a full-time mum. Things did improve for Sue when she employed a nanny two days per week. The nanny took Sue and the children to some local toddler groups and play facilities and Sue realised that she lacked confidence as a parent and felt that because of her circumstances she had to be 'beyond criticism'. She also realised that her fears of being criticised had adversely affected her confidence throughout her life and that she had avoided developing a life and career for herself and that she was very reliant on Stella. Sue began to take evening classes and started to look at herself in a whole new way. For Sue the transition to parenthood had caused a fundamental re-evaluation of her identity.

Post-natal depression and loss

The transition to parenthood involves the loss of many things: for women their working life changes, their body changes and, more fundamentally, how they see themselves changes. There are changes for new fathers and the couple too, particularly in terms of their social life and their finances. Many of these changes involve a sense of loss. Often this may coincide with or reawaken unresolved feelings of grief.

Janet's story

Janet came to see me following the birth of her third child. She said that it was the most enormous struggle to drag herself out of bed in the morning and if it wasn't for the fact that her husband was able to drop her two older children at school, she doubted that they would get there at all. Janet said that she couldn't understand why she was being such a 'waste of space' since usually she was a very capable person. Janet did

> *eventually reflect that it had been a difficult year. Her father had died suddenly of a heart attack not long after she had become pregnant. She was terribly sad that he had not seen her baby. Her mother had no longer felt able to run the bakery that the couple had owned throughout their life and it had had to be sold. Janet had worked in the bakery throughout her life and all of the family were struggling to come to terms with the new situation.*

Do fathers get post-natal depression?

There is much research now that highlights the difficulties many fathers have in coming to terms with their new role. Many men do experience emotional difficulties in those early months and as in Karen and Colin's situation, often when one parent becomes depressed, the other then experiences emotional difficulties. As discussed in Chapter 3, although men are less likely than women to develop depression they may increase their consumption of drugs or alcohol, stay out of the home or experience any number of other difficulties in response to their new situation.

Craig's story

Craig was referred for help with depression that was affecting his training to be a doctor. His depression began following the separation from his girlfriend and his five-month-old child. She was adamant that the relationship was over although she was happy for him to see as much of his daughter as he wanted. The trigger for depression was not the separation itself but the unbelievable sense of failure he felt. He had come from a single parent family himself and his father had never acknowledged him. His father had many children, with various mothers and he had not maintained any relationship with Craig. His mother had found him difficult and he had ended up in care repeatedly. He had been determined not to make the same mistakes as his father whom he bitterly resented for his absence. However, now he felt he was repeating the mistakes his father had made and therefore Craig could no longer simply be mad at his father as he felt he too was letting down his child.

Getting help with post-natal problems

Admitting that something is wrong

The first step to getting help with post-natal problems is recognising that there is something wrong and that there are things that need to be changed about your situation. Most women do not like to admit that they are depressed, particularly so early on after the birth of their baby, and when there is such a great sense of expectation around them. When you have just had a baby, you can feel that the spotlight is really on you and that everyone is assessing how you are getting on. To hold your hand up and say 'Help, I'm not coping' or 'I'm really unhappy' can seem like too much of a failure.

For many women it takes a while to acknowledge that there is a problem. There is often the feeling that 'Well, I just need a good night's sleep' and everything will be OK. It may be that you are so consumed with anxiety about how the baby is doing or so preoccupied with trying to sort out a 'routine' for the baby that you fail to notice that you are crying every few moments.

Beginning to talk

The first step should always be to try and talk to someone whom you trust about how you are feeling. This might be your partner or a relative or friend. It may be that you can identify the source of the problem: perhaps you still have dissatisfaction about your birth that need to be talked through with someone, perhaps you just need a break away from the baby to get some sleep or phone a friend for a chat. However, these post-natal weeks seem to be a time when women find it difficult to reflect on their experience partly because there is so much new learning going on that there really isn't much time to think about how you are feeling. Sometimes it may be that you need to speak to a professional to have the time and space to sort out what the problems are.

Getting help

Many women will need extra support at this time and your GP, midwife or health visitor should all be able to offer information and support. The type of help you might need will vary from person to person so the best place to start is to sit down with someone else and try to identify your difficulties. Sorting out your difficulties may be something that you feel you can do for yourself or you may feel that you need the help of other professional or voluntary organisations. It may be that your partner has to explore these options because he is concerned about your well-being.

Self-help

The emphasis of this book has been about being aware and informed and, therefore, trying to prevent problems developing. However, if you do feel you are not coping or feeling fed-up with things you may find that Chapter 8 of this book 'Dealing with anxiety and depression' helps you to understand and approach the problem slightly differently. Part of getting rid of depression is about identifying what the actual problems are that you face and what the emotions, thoughts and feelings are that are holding you back from changing your situation. There are many problems that you usually cannot solve for yourself: ill health, poverty, poor housing, violence in another person or marital breakdown. There are always things that you can do to improve your situation but unfortunately depression doesn't let you think like that. Isolation is not good for new mothers but depression tells you 'I'm too fed-up to go anywhere new'. Organisations such as the National Childbirth Trust (NCT) provide opportunities to join groups and meet with other new mothers. Many local churches have 'mother and baby' groups and usually you can just turn up on the day without being a member.

Where depression has been a feature of your life for a long time, you may need to see a therapist who can help you to work on these ideas. It's always worth speaking to your GP to see if he or she can recommend a therapist either through the NHS or privately.

Health visitor support

Many health visitors are now specially trained in supporting and listening to new mothers. Some health visitors will ask you to fill out a questionnaire at around six weeks after the baby is born. This questionnaire, the Edinburgh Post-natal Depression Scale or EPDS, helps to identify women who are depressed or struggling. You may find that the questionnaire helps to open up the discussion about how you are feeling and is meant to convey to mothers that health visitors are interested in how you coping not just how the baby is doing. Your health visitor may be able to visit you regularly at home and give you some time and space to explore how you are feeling. Health visitors can also offer specific advice about other types of help you might need and may introduce you to, for example, a post-natal support group. If your problems seem more deep-rooted or where you have had previous emotional difficulties your health visitor may ask you to see your GP or suggest you see a member of the mental health services.

Support within the NHS

The health visitor and GP are the first line of contact within the health service and they will have access to other services where needed. Many GPs now have counsellors, community psychiatric nurses or psychologists working at the surgery who can become involved where necessary. They may offer individual or group therapy following an assessment. They may also recommend the support of voluntary organisations or groups.

The support of other mothers and parents

Most studies looking at depression in mothers highlight a lack of confiding relationship or social support as a feature of the problem. Being together with other mothers-to-be in pregnancy has also been shown to be effective in the prevention of post-natal problems. It can be very difficult if feeling depressed to think about going along to a mother-and-baby group or joining a post-natal support group but for the women who do take the step, it can be an incredibly supportive experience. It may be that you need to go and talk to someone first about how you are feeling and then maybe you will feel able to take that step.

There is a list of addresses of organisations on p. 181 that you may like to contact for specific types of support, for example, mother-and-baby groups.

Who can help?

The section on post-natal problems has highlighted a number of types of support but it is important perhaps to highlight the range of different people you may come into contact with and the services that you may be offered in the first six weeks.

Care of your baby

Your midwife may remain involved in your care for up to 28 days after the birth of your baby. In practice, they tend to hand over to the health visitor in the first couple of weeks if all is going well.

Your health visitor will carry out a 'new birth visit' within the first month. She will be there to hear all about your experiences so far and to explain her role with your family until your child goes to school. The health visitor will invite you to bring your baby to the Baby Clinic once you are able enough and here you can have the baby weighed and discuss your progress or any problems with the health visitor or GP. You will also be offered a programme of immunisation for the baby in due course.

At around eight weeks you will be offered a 'developmental check' or 'review' of your baby's progress with the GP or health visitor.

Support for you

You will be offered a 'post-natal check' with your GP at around six weeks to discuss your recovery and any concerns that you have about your own health: physical or emotional.

When you do feel that you are not coping, you may be offered extra support from your health visitor, possibly visits at home. Where problems are more deep-rooted you may need to speak to a counsellor or other mental health professional.

Organisations such as the National Childbirth Trust run many supportive post-natal groups or drop-in facilities where you can meet other new mothers.

Discussion points

1. Getting to know your baby. Try describing your baby as if you were describing him to a stranger. How do you think the baby takes after you/your partner: looks, personality? How does your baby let you know how he is feeling? Crying? Wriggling? Cooing? Does your baby have any routines/predictable patterns yet? Are there any concerns about your baby you feel you need to discuss with someone?
2. Are you feeling well? Do you feel you have physically recovered from the birth and, if not, what are the problems? How are you both doing in terms of sleeping, eating and relaxing?
3. Are there any concerns about how you are feeling?
4. Do you need any more help or support from others?

8

Managing anxiety and depression

The journey through pregnancy and into parenthood brings with it psychological risks. The previous chapters have outlined different types of psychological difficulties mothers might experience and why. The emphasis of this book has been about trying to prevent problems by being more aware and informed about the emotional pressures that you might experience when you embark upon having a family. However, for some women the events of pregnancy and childbirth will lead to significant levels of anxiety or depression or these may have been around for most of your life. Each chapter has tried to highlight issues specific to problems at that stage; such as the reasons for depression in pregnancy; what follows here are some *general* points about dealing with these problems whenever they occur.

Understanding and coping with stress and anxiety

Everyone experiences stress or anxiety at some point in his or her life. It is usually viewed as a problem but moderate levels of stress actually help us to perform better. If about to have an interview or raise a difficult issue with a friend, it is perfectly normal to feel 'butterflies' in your stomach or to breathe faster than usual. Our bodies are preparing us for action or to face perceived challenges. At times we have all felt 'panicky', been preoccupied with worries or avoided something we would rather not deal with.

However, when these signs become regular or intense or in the 'wrong' situation, then anxiety can be a cause of much dread and misery as well as being detrimental to health in the long term.

The aim of this chapter is 'coping' and 'understanding' NOT 'avoiding' anxiety. Many people I have worked with have wanted to know how to avoid the problem. Avoiding the problem only ever makes things worse in the long run. Anxiety can only be solved by learning to *cope with the symptoms* so that you can begin to *explore* and *understand the problems*. The following areas will be covered in this section:

1. What are the signs or symptoms of anxiety?
2. How does anxiety affect peoples' lives?
3. What causes these problems?
4. How can I cope with anxiety/manage my life better?

What do we mean by 'stress' or 'anxiety'?

Most people don't need to be told that they are under stress or what stress means to them. However, 'stress' is a word used in many contexts but generally refers to a situation where the demands that you experience in your everyday life outweigh the resources that you feel you have to cope with those demands.

Anxiety has also come to refer to many types of experiences. Here it will be used to refer to a type of problem or experience that can be divided into the following three aspects:

1. 'physical' – bodily experiences and sensations
2. 'thoughts' – negative thinking, fears, worries, tendency to catastrophise
3. 'behaviour' – avoidance of the situation or problem.

How do you know you are stressed?

The list of signs or symptoms is endless and each individual has their own unique set of experiences. Generally, these experiences fall into the following categories:

- chest pain or tight feeling across the chest
- palpitations
- dizziness
- sweating
- hot and cold flushes
- blushing

- shortness of breath
- hyperventilation
- difficulty swallowing
- shakiness/trembling
- tingling sensations
- tension; muscle cramps; aches and pains, especially backache and headache
- nausea
- dry mouth
- diarrhoea.

There are probably many other types of experience that you can add to the list. But what causes these physical symptoms? In order to understand, this it is helpful to look at what happens in a panic attack.

Understanding the reasons for bodily symptoms – the panic spiral

When we find ourselves in a situation that we perceive as threatening, our body prepares us for action: adrenaline starts to pump around the body and therefore our heart begins to race; breathing becomes more rapid. This is known as the *fight or flight response*. This physical response can be traced back to our prehistoric ancestors who needed to flee from predators. When you are stressed, your body goes into a state of high physical arousal and these bodily changes prepare us for action – to 'flee' from the situation or 'fight'. However, in a panic attack these symptoms occur in a situation where there is no obvious danger, such as on a train or at the supermarket. This we call a panic attack. An association is made that this situation is in some way threatening and the symptoms return whenever we return to a similar situation.

Karl's story

One morning as Karl stood on the platform waiting for his train to arrive, his heart began racing and he started to sweat heavily. He sat down on a bench as he thought he was having a heart attack. He remained there while the passengers boarded the train and when he felt a bit better, he managed to walk home and spent the day in bed. Next morning he went to the station as usual but found himself sweating profusely as he approached the platform and his heart began to race. He was convinced that he was on the verge of a heart attack and went straight to his GP. His GP sent him for various tests but eventually said he was physically quite well. Karl stayed away from work and was now terrified of going anywhere near the train station.

Karl needed help to manage his symptoms of panic. He gave up his job rather than face the journey to work. As he began to manage his panic attacks, Karl recognised that he had hated his job and had felt that his life was going nowhere. He needed to rethink the direction of his life and as he began to do this he gradually regained his confidence and eventually was able to use the train again.

Panic attacks can seem to come out of the blue but are generally a sign of an increasingly stressful situation or set of events. Naturally we interpret these symptoms as signs of something catastrophic, i.e.:

1. *'I'm going mad'*: some form of imminent psychological breakdown.
2. *'I'm having a heart attack'*: serious or fatal health problems.
3. *'I'm going to make a fool of myself'*: the fear of terrible loss of control/ embarrassment in front of others.

The natural reaction is to avoid the situation in which the feelings occurred: to get out of the meeting or leave the supermarket. However, the panic attack *will not harm you*. If you can stay in the situation, the panic will subside.

These three factors: physical symptoms, frightening thoughts and avoidance behaviour together create a vicious circle. The experience of panic is so frightening and unpleasant, there is usually a desperate attempt to avoid it happening again at all costs. Therefore, we tend to look for any physical changes; avoid the situations where it has taken place and fully believe the frightening thoughts that occurred during the panic: 'If the train stops in a tunnel, I'm sure I'll not be able to breathe and I'll collapse.'

Many people who come for help with anxiety problems are caught up in their 'fear of fear'. They are so terrified of panicking that they are constantly looking for signs that they might panic. When they feel like this, people will avoid any situation that has been associated with panic, any event or activity that might make their heart race, make them feel nervous or even avoid rushing for a bus in case it triggers a panic. Ironically when someone can get to the point where they can say 'I really don't care if I have a panic attack', this is the point where the panics will usually subside.

April's story

April, who was 28 years old, only managed to get to her first appointment with me because her mother had brought her. She had rarely been out of the house since she had given up her 'stressful' job as a travel agent, three months previously. She had been repeatedly panicking at work following an incident when a customer had become angry and abusive towards her. At first she had enjoyed the safety of being at home with her mother. However, now the symptoms had started to happen at home whenever her mother left the house. This had made life almost impossible for both of them since every time her mother went out April would become tearful and resentful.

April made significant progress by learning to face her panic and managing to go out again, starting with very small journeys. She also began to think about the underlying reasons for her anxiety. She had lived with just her mother since her father had left when she was five. It was very frightening for both April and her mother to think about her becoming an adult and leaving home at some point.

How does anxiety affect people's lives?

As well as the immediate and distressing symptoms of panic, anxiety can have more subtle or longer-term effects. These we would call the secondary symptoms of anxiety.

Changes in behaviour

- Sleep problems
- Appetite loss or over-eating
- Drinking/smoking/drug use
- Avoidance of certain situations/people/places/problems
- Over-activity/inactivity.

Changes in how we think

- Poor concentration
- Problems making decisions

- Memory problems
- Negative thinking/more rigid thinking.

Emotional changes

- Increase in a range of anxiety problems: panics, phobias, obsessions
- Increase in depression: sadness, apathy, fatigue
- Mood swings
- Problems with anger/irritability/aggression.

Effects on health

- Can cause or worsen certain health problems such as hypertension or asthma
- Digestive problems
- General feelings of ill health.

What causes anxiety problems?

- Stress is a very individual experience, therefore the sources of stress for any individual will be different.
- Sources of stress can be everyday demands or major life changes.
- Every aspect of life can be a source of stress for a particular individual at a particular time.

Here are a few examples:

- Family life: raising children, looking after an older relative or grand-children; marital breakdown, interpersonal disputes, moving house.
- Work: work overload, unemployment, problems with colleagues, financial problems.
- Illness and disability.
- Accidents and trauma.
- Personal/developmental: boredom, lack of personal fulfilment or direction, few interests.

Research has shown that the more of these life events we experience, the more likely we are to experience stress. Also we are not just talking about negative events, positive changes can also bring stress: getting married, having a baby, moving house, Christmas and holidays can all bring stress.

Overall, then, it is our ability to *adapt and change* in response to these events in life that will predict how much stress we experience. Adapting to life events can mean having to let go of the past, possibly facing a period of uncertainty and self-doubt. It may mean learning new skills or being open to new ideas. Research shows that if you can embrace and enjoy change, then you will experience less stress. Therefore, what changes can we make to manage life differently and therefore reduce our stress?

'How can I cope with anxiety/manage my life differently?'

Once you have started to identify signs and sources of stress in your life, you will have already gone a long way towards dealing with them. It is important to believe that you can change and not allow these feelings to overwhelm you and make you feel powerless.

Below is a list of ways of tackling stress and life problems generally. Try out different things as some may be more helpful to you than others.

Identify and understand your symptoms

- Keep a *stress diary* and monitor when, where and how you are feeling stressed. Look for patterns of symptoms or particular situations that bring them on (see Designing Diaries on p. 186).
- Check out with your doctor anything that you feel might be undiagnosed ill health.
- If you have anxiety symptoms (fight and flight as discussed earlier), try to follow the steps outlined below:

Learning to cope with feelings of panic

- Relaxation: learn the techniques of relaxation so that you can put these into action before you start to panic (see the relaxation cassette discussed on p. 188). Try to visualize relaxing scenes.
- Monitor your panic thoughts. As you learn about what is happening to your body in a panic, try to recognise that what you are saying to yourself increases the panic: 'I'm going to faint'; 'I'm going to run screaming from the cinema', etc.

- Positive self-talk: try to replace these panic thoughts with more rational ones: 'my breathing will slow down if I sit down for a minute'. Or focus on the word 'calm'.
- Distraction: think of a very relaxing place, listen to some music, count backwards from 100 – whatever works for you!
- Do not avoid or leave a panic situation: the feelings will go away quickly but will be worse next time. If you stay in the situation, the symptoms will eventually subside, as the feared catastrophe does not occur.

If you have been avoiding this problem for some time, you will need to start by identifying the situations that you have been avoiding and gradually face these events, starting with the least feared ones first.

Identify sources of stress

Take a realistic look at what you can change and what you cannot. Remember you *cannot change other people*; you can only change yourself and your own way of life.

Don't try to tackle everything at once: start with things that are easy to change, then you can build on your success.

Learn new life skills and ways of coping

See the section below on depression.

Understanding and coping with depression

In the previous chapters it has been highlighted that depression can be experienced throughout the life cycle but that becoming pregnant and having and caring for a baby may be times when women and their partners experience periods of depression. In previous chapters the experience or symptoms of depression have been looked at and there was also discussion of some of the things that might lead to depression at these times: a labour that wasn't what you were expecting, a sense of loss for former aspects of your life, a poor relationship with your own parents, and so on.

You should always go and see your doctor if feeling depressed and try and get as much help and support as possible. Depending on the nature of your difficulties, the doctor may recommend various treatments – possibly medication or that you should see a counsellor or therapist or he or she might just monitor your progress. You might also get support from your family, friends or your church.

As well as seeking help from a professional, there are ways that you can begin to understand and cope with your depression and some of these ideas are introduced below. You can use these ideas while taking medication, while waiting to see a therapist or alongside any other supportive discussions that you might be having. If you are referred to see a counsellor or therapist, you can tell them about any self-help work you have been doing. This will help you to decide together what needs to be done next.

Challenging depression

Some of the factors that contribute to people's depression cannot be changed: if you are living in extreme poverty, if you had a complicated labour or a very poor experience of parenting in your own childhood, then these factors in themselves cannot be changed. However, there usually are aspects of your depression that can be changed. People do recover from awful experiences and depression is not inevitable and this is partly to do with how they view themselves and the world around them. For example, a child who is bullied at school may grow up to feel that he is 'not someone that people like' or 'not someone that people want to be friends with' and therefore he is less likely to try to make new friends or change his situation. His lack of a social life confirms his belief about himself and means he is isolated, has no-one to confide in and is more likely to be depressed. Another child who was bullied at school may think that the children picked on him for a specific reason: because he wore glasses or joined the class later in the year, for example, and that the children were inadequate in some way themselves if they needed to bully him. He may have learnt from this that he needed to be tougher and more determined to put his point of view across. This may mean that as an adult he is much more assertive because of the experience.

Therefore, bad life experiences do not necessarily mean that we will get depressed (obviously, though, the more bad things that happen to you, the more difficult it is to keep being positive). Partly it is how we attribute meaning to what has happened.

Research has shown that people can improve their depression by tackling some of the negative thoughts and feelings that contribute to keeping us depressed. The ideas presented below are meant to help you explore and understand your feelings of depression.

Step 1: 'Why am I depressed at the moment?' Identifying problems

One of the reasons that sadness turns into depression is because people fail to understand why they are feeling unhappy or what exactly their problems are. Sometimes people have been feeling slightly depressed for most of their life. Therefore, the most important step to getting rid of depression is trying to understand the reasons that it happened. Depression changes the way we think and feel and usually when we are depressed we do not stop and think about what is happening to us.

Keeping a diary

When you are feeling depressed, life can just rattle on in a monotonous way: you are feeling miserable but haven't really got the energy to try to understand what your depression might be about. This is why it is extremely useful to keep a diary of your thoughts and feelings. You can do this in whichever way you like but it helps if you decide on what you are going to record, otherwise it can become too onerous a task.

One useful way, similar to the drinking diary in Chapter 3, is to try and record the following information every time you feel low or upset by something:

1. Triggers/situation: what was happening, what you were doing, who was there, any incident that might have caused you to feel low or upset.
2. Thoughts and feelings: what was going through your mind at the time? How were you thinking and feeling?
3. Consequences: what did you do next/in response to these thoughts or feelings?

This might then read: (1) Monday p.m. – lying in bed trying to get to sleep; (2) thinking about the day ahead tomorrow, wondering if I will be able to cope, feeling guilty for having been so cross with the children today; (3) was awake for a long time and felt even worse the next day.

Just keep the diary for a week or two in the first instance. Don't allow the diary to become a chore. Carry on with it if you find it really helpful.

What's the point in keeping a diary?

There are lots of other things that you might like to record or different ways that you could do it. You may feel depressed all of the time, if so, then you could just record incidents where you feel worse or upset or even when you feel a bit better. The idea of the task is to try to learn something about your depression.

Quite often when I set this task for people they come back saying they couldn't do it because they're only just coping with all they have to do or they are just too depressed to think. They inevitably see this as a failure and this confirms their belief that they are 'useless'. However, you can learn something even from an empty diary. What stopped you doing it? How did that make you feel about yourself? Useless? Fed-up? Feeling like a failure? This is the depression 'talking'. This is one of the things we are looking for in the diary: how the depressed part of us affects how we see the world. Through exploration of why the diary wasn't done, how you felt about the task and what thoughts and beliefs this reveals about yourself, you can learn an awful lot about your depression.

What am I looking for?

There are almost an infinite number of things that can be learned from a diary and everyone seems to find out something different. Some of the things that you might look at are as follows:

1. Things that might be generating the problems, patterns that emerge from the diary. 'Whenever I stay at my parents' house we end up arguing and I feel depressed the next day'. 'Whenever the baby has been feeding a lot I start to feel worried that the baby isn't getting enough milk, that I'm not doing it right and eventually everyone will realise I'm not capable of looking after a baby.' 'At the station when I wait for the train to work in the mornings, the panic starts.'
2. Are there common thoughts that accompany these situations?: 'I'm going to embarrass myself'; 'I'm not as good as...(or as clever as, as thin as, as pretty as...)', and so on. Here you are trying to identify critical or negative thinking: 'Clare never seems stressed with her baby, she's a perfect mother.'
3. Are you allowing your depression and negative thinking to restrict and control your life?: 'I didn't phone Clare and ended up feeling lonely all afternoon.'

What do I do next?

Well, that really depends on what you find out from your diary! If your diary has identified some triggers for your depression, then you may need to explore these situations in more depth. Are there unresolved issues in your relationship with your partner, a parent or colleague? If your diary is full of negative and self-defeating thinking, it may be that this is causing your depression and you may need to learn to change this (see later section on challenging negative thoughts). Have you stopped doing things that give you pleasure or a sense of achievement? Often depression can manifest itself in the 'tired all the time' syndrome. People explain their avoidance of activities as being due to tiredness and this avoidance leads to a less enjoyable life and more of a negative sense of self or lack of purpose. If you are caring for a new baby and getting up at night, you may well justifiably feel tired all of the time but do try and make some time for yourself to do something that you enjoy, even if it is just reading the newspaper for half-an-hour.

It may be that after identifying some problems that you feel a bit stuck. If so, try to sit down with someone you trust and discuss what you have found out. You can ask them for their perspective: 'do you think I'm very critical of myself?' 'I feel depressed when my mother is around, what do you notice when she is here?' If you can't get any further perhaps now might be a time to seek out some professional help.

Step 2 looks at some general solutions to the sorts of problems that people identify as causing their depression. In reading through these, you may find some that seem to be right for you and your situation.

Step 2: Learning new skills

Problem solving

Often when people are depressed, they feel completely overwhelmed by their problems or find it difficult to identify what their problems are: 'I'm just feeling bad.' Hopefully if you have managed to keep a diary you will have begun to identify things that you need to change. Usually there are two reasons that people stop solving problems: first, they fail to identify what the problem is and, second, they set themselves too complicated a goal.

So, first, when identifying the problem, try to sort out what you can change and what you cannot: if you are fed-up with a lack of support at home because your partner has a very demanding job, then how can you get support from him when he is there? Who else can support you? What are the specific things that you need? Is it someone to talk to or someone to take the baby out for an hour while you have a sleep?

Try to make a list of all the things that you think would make you feel better and how you might go about achieving these. Try to be realistic: don't try to be the perfect mother, just try to be good enough.

Set yourself some goals

One way of moving forward is to try and set yourself some targets or goals. These goals need to be simple, achievable and realistic. If you have been very depressed for some time a realistic goal might be to phone a friend or get out of bed before lunchtime. If you set complicated or unrealistic goals: 'I want to change my career and be earning £30,000 by the time I am 25', you may well reinforce your sense of failure. Goals also need to be measurable, so that you can tell whether you have achieved them or not. For example: 'I need to be more assertive', is too vague. Break this down into a number of easily achievable steps: 'I want to say "no" once to my friend when she asks me to look after her children.' The next time she asks, you will know whether or not you have achieved that first step. If you don't achieve the goal, then break it down into smaller steps. If you ended up saying 'yes' to your friend again, then next time set yourself the goal of saying 'Yes, but I can only have the children for an hour because I have to go out later'.

Once you get going on the small steps, then the big challenges gradually become more achievable.

Expressing feelings/dealing with anger/assertiveness

It has been argued that depression can result from problems of dealing with powerful feelings such as anger. It is certainly true that when people are depressed they can have a number of strong feelings and thoughts that feel jumbled up and in need of unravelling. Learning to be more open and willing to discuss problems and feelings can help to resolve those problems and release pent-up anger and tension. Sometimes people need specific help with managing their anger but more often than not it is the exploration of the problems that are generating these feelings that lead to the feelings resolving. Often people fear that they will lose control or 'explode' with rage if they begin to talk but this is rarely the case.

We all deal with anger in different ways but if you think that you never get angry, then perhaps you need to think again. How do you deal with life's frustrations? Often it can feel easier to say nothing about small irritations but these can simmer away causing a great deal of stress and possibly boil over in a destructive way.

Roza's story

Roza was referred to see me for help with managing a chronic pain problem. She had a pain in her ankle that at times stopped her from walking. The doctors could find no clear cause for this pain and felt that she needed to learn some relaxation techniques. Roza had four children, two of whom were at school but her eldest son had recently started 'staying home' and she was finding it difficult to get him out of bed in the mornings. Roza had come to live in England to marry her husband who was born in this country. He had worked in the family catering business for many years but had not worked for three years since he had fallen out with his father. He usually stayed in bed until after she had taken the children to school. Roza was responsible for the care of the children and the housework. She said it would be inappropriate for a man to help her with these tasks but she did wish she had more support particularly concerning managing their eldest son's behaviour.

Roza expressed no anger or frustration towards her husband and said she was very sympathetic to his plight. However, she said that since her leg troubles she had suggested that he would have to walk the children to school as she often could not stand on her foot in the mornings.

Many people come for help with depression and realise that they need to be more assertive and say 'no' more because the cost is too high if they don't. However, this is always a difficult choice to make since it comes at a cost. When people are used to you behaving in a particular way, they don't want you to change. For Roza there were complicated cultural pressures and personal expectations about a relationship that made it hard for her to ask her husband for help. Learning to be more assertive is something that needs to be practised and often when you try to change your behaviour, the people around you only intensify their behaviour because they want you to stay the same. If you really want to change, then start with an easy situation and practise saying 'no'. After all are you really helping your family if you are left completely exhausted and irritable by their demands?

Identifying and challenging negative thinking

So, how we deal with our feelings and problems may be an aspect of becoming depressed. Research has also identified that depressed people are prone to thinking negatively about themselves and their life. This seems to be particularly apparent when faced by new challenges or difficult situations: 'I'll never do this as well as the others.' This negative thinking seems to reflect an underlying set of negative beliefs about themselves. Basically, 'my life is going badly because I am a useless person' or a 'bad' person or 'stupid'. You may not be aware of holding such beliefs about yourself or even that you are prone to thinking negatively. This is often because this is such a habitual way of thinking that you don't notice it. It is often keeping a diary that makes someone realise that they are making life twice as hard for themselves. If you are constantly criticising yourself and predicting failure, then you make it very hard to succeed at anything. Try to become more aware of negative thinking (use your diary to monitor your thoughts) if you keep saying 'I'm useless at this' then you are likely to feel stressed, demoralised and give up easily. Try to replace them with more helpful thoughts: 'If I keep practising, I'm sure I'll get the hang of it.'

Changing the way that you view yourself certainly can be an immense undertaking and not something that you can do overnight. If negative thinking appears to be a big factor in why you get depressed, then you might find it useful to look at one of the self-help books listed in the Further reading on p. 188.

Self-care

When experiencing either anxiety or depression it is very important to learn or relearn how to look after yourself. Depression may be a psychological problem but it is more difficult to have a healthy mind in an unhealthy body. As previously mentioned, feeling 'tired all the time' or unable to initiate activities is all part of being depressed. Again, try to start off with an easy step: it might be, for example, cutting out coffee or alcoholic drinks (particularly important for those with anxiety problems). People often falsely believe that these drinks make them feel better, either calmer or more awake but in fact they contribute to the experience of anxiety symptoms even in fairly moderate doses.

Activity and exercise are important factors in trying to recover from depression. Very often depression makes you lethargic and yet restless. Some form of activity or exercise can be an important first step in breaking out of this. Again, don't set yourself unrealistic goals: 'I can't do anything at the moment because I'm not able to afford membership of the gym.' Just going out for a walk to the local shop every morning can give you a boost of energy. Exercise can be a very important factor for many women after having a baby. Most women are keen to return to their pre-pregnancy state but may find it difficult to make time to go for a swim or do the things they did before they had a baby. Walking with the baby in the pram instead of driving everywhere is good for both of you. Going for a walk can help you in the early days to set a routine with the baby or to settle him if he is fretful.

Often women give their lives over to their baby in the early days and it may be important for you to identify some time for you to take care of or nurture yourself. That might mean a meal out or a relaxing bath or a trip to the hairdresser, whatever makes you feel a bit better or special.

Relearning how to enjoy yourself and feeling a sense of achievement

Enjoyment and a sense of personal fulfilment are two aspects of life that tend to disappear when someone is depressed. When depressed, people tend to avoid certain social situations or friends because they feel they will 'spoil it for others' or because they don't want people to know that they are depressed. We all need to enjoy ourselves, to have contact with other people and to feel that we do some worthwhile things. Consequently, this avoidance makes us feel even more depressed.

When setting yourself some goals, it is really important to identify at least one activity that you can start to try doing again. When you have been very depressed, this may need to be a very small step initially. You might just want to call a friend, take a walk through the park, or make a shopping trip. This will help your depression in other ways too. Often when people are depressed, their lives lack structure and they find it difficult to initiate activities. After having a baby you may feel your day is completely full up but try and make some space to do just one special thing for yourself each day.

As well as trying to have some positive social experiences, it is also important to remind yourself of what you are good at. Make a list of things that give you a sense of achievement and look at trying to reintroduce some of these into your life. Again, where you have been very depressed you may feel you aren't good at anything. Your initial objective should therefore be a small easily achievable goal, even if it is just reading a magazine, so that you can look back at the end of the day and feel you have achieved your task for the day.

After having a baby, particularly if you had a very active life before, depression can manifest itself in an enormous amount of frustration about what you cannot achieve now that you have a baby. The important factor here is really about adjusting to your new situation and accepting that for the moment things have to be different. If you have no expectations of having free time, then every time your baby goes to sleep it will be a bonus. However, if you start the day hoping to clean up the house, make dinner, catch up on some phone calls and sort out your paperwork, then you are likely to continually feel frustrated. 'Time management' is not about being shown the secret way of trying to fit more things into your day, it is about trying to be realistic and prioritising your tasks so that you do what you really have to and don't keep 'beating yourself up' about what you haven't achieved.

Deciding to change

Nobody wants to be depressed or gripped by fears and panics but moving away from these symptoms can be a frightening prospect. Once you have accepted that there is no magic wand and you cannot simply have your depression or anxiety 'taken away', you will begin to realise that you need to make changes if you are to get better. These will be different for each person. This might mean recognising your role in your relationship problems or deciding that you have to confront a difficult situation. In order to tackle your anxiety problems you may need to start going back to situations that you have avoided. Sometimes with all these challenges it can seem easier to do nothing and just hope that soon it will all go away. Sometimes you need help to motivate yourself to do anything differently. Try setting yourself the task of imagining life if you do not change. Try to write a description of your life in five years' time if you continue to be depressed. What will you be doing? Where will you be living? What will family life be like? Alternatively, try to write a list of everything that you feel your depression or anxiety stops you from doing. What things have you missed out on in life since you have had these problems? Have you avoided taking career moves, lost contact with friends, missed out on social events, and so on? Then make a list of any of the positive benefits of being like this. For example, 'I get to avoid another argument with my partner', 'I don't have to feel uncertain' or 'I don't risk feeling optimistic and then being disappointed.' Take a look at the benefits of staying the same and ask yourself if these outweigh the benefits of change.

Looking forward from depression and anxiety

The different ideas in this chapter may all seem very complicated at the moment and it is important to remember that you can take just one step at a time. When you have had a baby there is an enormous amount of change going on and it may take you some time to catch up with the changes. Sometimes when things are getting a bit better, you may experience a setback and then feel even more hopeless. The early days of trying to change can be very difficult so try to rally as much support as possible when things become difficult.

Who can help?

Experiencing stress, especially panic and anxiety symptoms, can be extremely distressing and demoralising. Trying to do something about it requires a lot of hard work at a time where you probably feel least able to find the energy. However, you may find that taking the first few steps can bring an enormous sense of relief and quite quickly you may feel hopeful about changing your life. If you can't get going on your own, speak to your GP who should be able to recommend a psychologist, counsellor or possibly an anxiety management course. There are also self-help organisations that run groups or offer individual support over the phone (see the list of addresses on p. 181). Many local councils also run 'stress management' courses within their adult education programme. Always try as many different options as you can to try and find the right one for you.

9

The journey that never ends

Looking ahead

In the course of a year you will have made an incredible transition from an individual to expectant parent through to a family. You are now the parent of a baby who is growing and developing rapidly. When you look back, you will probably wish you had done certain things differently and wonder why you didn't realise other things. Hopefully, though, the pleasures will have outweighed the disappointments. If you have had a difficult or disappointing time, then it is perhaps important to remember that the relationship between mother and baby is not a static one: it is constantly changing and evolving. If you have struggled in the first six weeks, this doesn't mean that you are doomed to be a bad parent or that your baby will always be unsettled or whatever your worry may be. No one is a 'perfect mother' or gets it right all of the time. Clearly, some parents find it easier, and some infants offer more complex challenges.

Often as soon as you have established a routine with your baby, or feel that you are getting on top of things, a new challenge comes along: perhaps your baby catches a cold and his feeding and sleeping go awry. Outside events may change your situation: your partner loses his job or a close relative dies. Suddenly you have to deal with the outside world again and manage your own and your baby's life around these new circumstances. Just as you will experience further life events, so too will your baby. This can come as a bit of a shock for parents who hope that they can simply avoid their baby ever being frustrated or upset. For example, your baby might develop eczema and your usually content baby may become distressed and frustrated. You will have to help him manage this experience. Separations can also be difficult for mothers and babies. If you return to work, you will have to leave your baby in the care of someone else and deal with the feelings that this stirs up in you and with the feelings and reactions it generates in your baby. Even if you don't return to work, your baby will have to learn to manage at times without you there.

Donald Winnicott introduced the idea of the 'good enough' mother and that is what we should be aiming for. As with any relationship, you cannot always get it right and at times there will be misunderstandings, disagreements or external pressures that make your relationship with your baby difficult or unpredictable. Sometimes you will have to wait and tolerate uncertainty until you work out the way forward together. It is important to remember this as you struggle with each new challenge. If your baby wakes frequently at night after months of 'sleeping through', if he cries a lot because he is frustrated in his attempts to crawl or if he refuses to give up the breast, then it may take time for a solution to develop and you may have to tolerate distress in your baby and yourself.

The new 'me'

This process of development continues for all of the family and each developmental stage brings new challenges. Often it may feel as if nothing stays the same for long: as soon as a family has found some equilibrium or routine, then the baby develops and everything changes again.

These developmental changes are more apparent in the baby: as he begins to take solid food or begins to crawl. However, the changes are continuing for you too. You can never really return to the same place as before. Even if you take a short maternity leave and return to the same job, it will feel different when you have a baby. Having to leave your baby stirs up complicated emotions but also, on a practical level, it makes life more complicated. Your priorities are split. In time you may have more children, your baby will become a toddler and eventually go to school. All along he will need you but in different ways at different times.

In becoming a parent, your view of yourself will have changed. Now you are 'mother' and 'parent' as well as all the other roles that you may perform. As you move into these roles you will be continually faced by dilemmas over priorities. Again, it is about finding what is right for you and your family. For some women, over time that might bring a recognition of having made sacrifices: perhaps missing out on times with your child or perhaps having given up the idea of holding the 'top job' at work.

Looking ahead you probably don't want to miss out in any areas but what is important is to make your own decisions over time.

For many fathers, especially those who have been less involved early on, feeling that you have become a father may take a long time. Finding your role as a father can often be difficult, especially where a mother is breast-feeding for long periods of time. This role may develop more slowly and it may seem difficult to be still making mistakes if the mother seems so competent and keeps telling the father what to do. Some fathers may have taken a much more active role especially if a mother has struggled with post-natal depression. Becoming a father may have made the partner review his own 'life plan' too. He may ask himself, 'Do I want to be away from the home so much as I used to? How can I become more involved in family life?'

The journey for your family continues with all its ups and downs. With good communication between all of you, hopefully the journey will be unforgettable.

Addresses of useful organisations

British Acupuncture Council
020 8735 0400
www.acupuncture.org.uk

British Pregnancy Advisory Service
Helpline 0845 730 40 30
www.bpas.org.uk

Child Bereavement Trust
01494 446 648
www.childbereavement.org.uk
Information and support for parents and children who have lost a family member.

Contact a Family
0808 808 3555
www.cafamily.org.uk
Information and support for families caring for a child with disabilities. Support group contacts.

Cruse
Helpline 0870 167 1677
www.crusebereavementcare.org.uk
For advice, individual and group counselling for bereavement.

Eating Disorders Association
Helpline 0845 634 1414
www.edauk.com

Foundation for the Study of Infant Deaths
Helpline 0870 787 0554
www.sids.org.uk

Independent Midwives Association
01483 821104
www.independentmidwives.org.uk

Infertility Network U.K.
01424 732361
www.child.org.uk
Support for those experiencing fertility problems or undergoing treatment.

Meet-a-Mum Association (MAMA)
Helpline 01525 217064
www.mama.org.uk
Provides advice and support to new mothers. Network of support groups
around the country.

Miscarriage Association
Helpline 01924 200799
www.the-ma.org.uk

National Childbirth Trust
Helpline 0870 444 8707
Breast-feeding helpline 0870 444 8708
www.nct-online.org
The NCT provides a wide range of services to families including
parenting classes, post-natal support groups and a range of local
events.

NHS Direct
0845 46 47
www.nhsdirect.nhs.uk
For information or non-urgent queries about your health or your baby's
health.

NHS Pregnancy Smoking Helpline
0800 169 0 169
www.givingupsmoking.co.uk

No Panic
Free phone 0808 808 0545
www.nopanic.org.uk
Information, telephone support and local groups for anxiety problems.

Relate
For telephone enquiries, see a local telephone directory for a local contact number.
www.relate.org.uk
Relate offer counselling for relationship problems and sexual problems.

SANDS (Stillbirth and Neonatal Death Society)
Helpline 020 7436 5881 or 7940
www.uk-sands.org
Support for parents and families whose baby is stillborn or dies shortly after birth.

Serene (formerly Cry-sis)
Helpline 020 7404 5011
BM Serene Crysis. London.WC1N 3XX
Helpline for parents whose children cry a great deal.

The Society of Homeopaths
01604 621400
www.homeopathy-soh.org

Twins and Multiple Birth Association (TAMBA)
0870 770 3305
www.tamba.org.uk

Designing diaries:
Anxiety, depression, drinking

When you want to change something in your life such as the amount of alcohol you are drinking or if you want to monitor your experience of depression, then it can be useful to keep a 'diary'. The examples below show you how you might record this information. You really can do this any way that you find helpful. You might just want to write down a record of your day but it can be useful to divide up your page into columns and record the same information every time you feel anxious or every time you have a drink.

Drinking diary

Where you were	Reason for drinking	Alternative action
Just got home from work	Felt stressed, fed up, row with colleague Sarah	Could have had a bath, could have phoned Sarah
Friend's house for dinner	Long evening, felt nervous	Should have left, tried to talk to someone

Diary to record anxiety or panic attacks

What was happening?	*How did you feel?*	*What did you do next?*
Going into shopping centre	Started to sweat, heart racing, felt sick	Couldn't go in so drove to local shop

Diary to record negative thoughts

Triggering event/ situation	*How were you feeling?*	*Negative thoughts*
Baby crying	Felt anxious that she might be ill, also tired and fed up	I can't phone the doctor again or they'll think I'm completely useless as a mother
Bought new dress and showed to friends	Depressed	Think I look fat, sure they are laughing at me

References

References

Belsky, J. (2001) Emanuel Miller Lecture: developmental risks (still) associated with early childcare. *Journal of Child Psychology and Psychiatry,* **42**, 845–59.

Blair, P.S., Fleming, P.J., Smith, I.J., Platt, M.W., Young, J., Nadin, P., *et al.* (1999) Babies sleeping with parents: case-control study of factors influencing the risk of the sudden infant death syndrome. *British Medical Journal,* **319**, 1457–62.

Clement, S.,Wilson, J. and Sikorski, J. (1998) Women's experiences of antenatal ultrasound scans. In Clement, S. (ed.) *Psychological Perspectives on Pregnancy and Childbirth.* Edinburgh: Churchill Livingstone.

Daws, D. (1985) Sleep problems in babies and young children. *Journal of Child Psychotherapy,* **11**, 87–95.

Evans, J., Heron, J., Francomb, H., Oke, S. and Golding, J. (2001) Cohort study of depressed mood during pregnancy and after childbirth. *British Medical Journal,* **323**, 257–60.

Ford, G. (2002) *The New Contented Little Baby Book.* London: Vermilion.

General Psychiatry Section Working Party on Postnatal Mental Illness (1992) Report of the General Psychiatry Section Working Party on postnatal mental illness. *Psychiatric Bulletin,* **16**, 519–22.

Health Education Authority (1997) *The Pregnancy Book.* London: Health Education Authority.

Johanson, R., Chapman, G., Murray, D., Johnson, I. and Cox, J. (2000) The North Staffordshire Maternity Hospital prospective study of pregnancy-associated depression. *Journal of Psychosomatic, Obstetrics and Gynaecology,* **21**, 93–7.

Kaye, K. (1982) *The Mental and Social Life of Babies: How Parents Create Persons.* Chicago: University of Chicago Press.

Kendell, R.E., McGuire, R.J., Connor, Y. and Cox, J. (1981) Mood changes in the first three weeks after childbirth. *Journal of Affective Disorders,* **3**, 317–26.

Kumar, R. and Robson, K.M. (1984) A prospective study of emotional disorders in childbearing women. *British Journal of Psychiatry,* **144**, 35–47.

Murray, L. and Andrews, L. (2000) *The Social Baby.* Surrey: The Children's Project Ltd.

Thomas, A. and Chess, S. (1977) *Temperament and Development.* New York: Brunner/Mazel.

Winnicott, D.W. (1988) *Babies and their Mothers.* London: Free Association Books.

Further reading

Eating problems

Bulimia Nervosa and Binge Eating: A Guide to Recovery by Peter Cooper and Chris Fairburn (London: Constable Robinson, 1993).

Getting Better Bit (e) by Bit (e): A Survival Kit for Sufferers of Bulimia Nervosa and Binge Eating Disorders by Ulrike Schmidt and Janet Treasure (Hove: Psychology Press, 1993).

Anorexia Nervosa: A Survival Guide for Families, Friends and Sufferers by Janet Treasure (Hove: Psychology Press, 1997).

Depression

Overcoming Depression by Paul Gilbert (London: Constable Robinson, 2000).

Postnatal Depression by Paula Nicolson (Chichester: John Wiley & Sons, 2001).

Anxiety

Cognitive Therapy of Anxiety by Adrian Wells (Chichester: John Wiley & Sons, 1997).

Managing Your Mind: The Mental Fitness Guide by Gillian Butler and Tony Hope (Oxford: Oxford University Press, 1997).

Survivors of childhood sexual abuse

The Courage to Heal: A Guide for Women Survivors of Child Sexual Abuse by Ellen Bass and Laura Davis (London: Vermilion, 2002).

Breaking Free: Help for Survivors of Child Sexual Abuse by Carolyn Ainscroft and Kay Toon (London: Sheldon Press, 2002).

I Never Told Anyone: Writings by Women Survivors of Child Sexual Abuse by Ellen Bass and Louise Thornton (eds) (New York: HarperPerennial, 1991).

Obsessive compulsive disorder

Obsessive Compulsive Disorder: Theory, Research and Treatment by Ross Menzies and Padmal De Silva (Chichester: John Wiley & Sons, 2003).

Relaxation

Complete Relaxation (audiobook) by Glenn Harrold (Diviniti Publishing Ltd, 2000).

The Relaxation and Stress Reduction Workbook by Martha Davis, Elizabeth Robbins Eshelman and Mathew McKay (Oakland, CA: New Harbinger Publications, 2000).

Index